THE
FUTURE
OF US

DESTINY IMAGE BOOKS BY JULIA LOREN

Supernatural Anointing

Shifting Shadows of Supernatural Power

Shifting Shadows of Supernatural Experiences

The

FUTURE

of Us

*Your Guide to Prophecy, Prayer,
and the Coming Days*

JULIA LOREN

with

**Bill Johnson • Heidi Baker
James Goll • Brennan Manning
Rick Joyner** • Mahesh Chavda
F.F. Bosworth • C Peter Wagner
Julie Meyer • Leanne Payne
Sharon Stone • Martin Scott
Shawn Bolz • David Demain

DESTINY IMAGE® PUBLISHERS, INC.
P.O. Box 310, Shippensburg, PA 17257-0310
"Promoting Inspired Lives."

This book and all other Destiny Image, Revival Press, MercyPlace, Fresh Bread, Destiny Image Fiction, and Treasure House books are available at Christian bookstores and distributors worldwide.

For a U.S. bookstore nearest you, call 1-800-722-6774.
For more information on foreign distributors, call 717-532-3040.
Reach us on the Internet: www.destinyimage.com.

ISBN 13 TP: 978-0-7684-0336-7
ISBN 13 Ebook: 978-0-7684-8565-3

For Worldwide Distribution, Printed in the U.S.A.
1 2 3 4 5 6 7 8 / 18 17 16 15 14

CONTENTS

Part 3 How to Change the World

Book Disclaimer

The opinions expressed by the contributors and those quoted are theirs alone, and do not reflect the opinions of the other contributors or of various readers. The contributing authors are not necessarily endorsing either the views or the ministries of all other contributors.

The information provided in this book is designed to provide helpful information on the subjects discussed. This book is not meant to be used, nor should it be used, to influence your life decisions. Predictive and futuristic words and views by any one minister should never be utilized in real-world decisions. Take them to prayer and listen on your own.

This book is designed to provide information and motivation to our readers. It is sold with the understanding that the author and the publisher is not engaged to render any type of psychological, legal, or any other kind of professional advice. The content of each article is the sole expression and opinion of its author, and not necessarily that of the author, publisher, or of the other contributors. No warranties or guarantees are expressed or implied by the author's choice to include any of the content in this volume. Neither the publisher nor the individual author(s)/contributors shall be liable for any physical, psychological, emotional, financial, or commercial damages, including, but not limited to, special, incidental, consequential, or other damages. Our views and rights are the same: You are responsible for your own choices, actions, and results.

*God has not given us a spirit of fear,
but of love, power, and a sound mind.*

During the recession of 1975, Kathryn Khulman spoke in Las Vegas about how dark and uncertain the times were. The times haven't changed—the days ahead are still uncertain and certainly full of shifting shadows. Her comment still rings true: "What the world needs is not something the Democrats or Republicans can give to us. What the world needs is a fresh baptism of the Love of God."

We do need a fresh baptism of God's love—poured out around the world. Many of the prophetic words contained in this book speak about a coming awakening to God's love. They are promises of what is to come. In the meanwhile, they also call us to be an extension of God's love to others—today!

In this book, I purposely steer clear of conspiracy theories, end-times chatter, wars and rumors of wars, and words of global economic collapse, doom, or gloom. However, I do address natural disasters for they have significant impact and they are something guaranteed to effect major populations in the years to come. I include them because I want to see us prepared and to rise up to bless the world. And no matter what happens in the world to come—such as economic and civil chaos—preparing for natural disasters will also aid in preparing for man-made disasters.

I believe that darkness and light will exist together until Jesus returns. What we choose to focus on multiplies in our lives. If you surrender to fear and live in fear, then God's love will seem far from you. If you focus on God's love, then fear will move far away. Perfect love casts out fear. Prayer should be centered in love and motivate us to move into our sacred destinies to become agents of change in our spheres of influence—not agents of fear.

The years to come will carry both the promise of amazing breakthroughs and horrendous disasters around the world that will impact individuals and whole nations. However, nothing is written in stone. Your future is partially in your control, dependent upon the choices you make today. The future of the nations is also in God's control and depends partly on the choices today's political and economic leaders make now. Our prayers are powerful and shape history. Together, our prayers can impact the world. And our actions can extend God's love in practical ways to transform those around us.

As you read this, keep in mind that the prophetic warnings of things to come serve as opportunities to plan ahead. Prophetic promises over the destiny of nations serve as opportunities to pray into the plans of God and act as God directs. Together, we can turn the tide of history. In fact, you were born during this hour of history for a reason. Listen to the voice of the Holy Spirit as you read, and perhaps you will feel some new direction, some new prayer or preparation you need to do to position yourself for purpose and prosper in the days ahead. Our prayers are powerful. No matter what happens, God is in the business of redemption. Jesus is in the "seek and save" business—not the "condemn and annihilate" business.

We all have a prophetic destiny. What is going to happen in your life and through your life to impact others has yet to be determined by you. What is going to happen in a nation and through a nation has yet to be determined. Global prayer movements are impacting whole regions. I write this to encourage you to come together with other followers of Jesus to pray in unity and faith. In the process, lives change, political decisions are brought into alignment with God's plans and purposes, angels are released, and blessings remove curses.

The future depends on you. It is my deepest wish that you read this book and discover who you are, how you can pray, and what you are called to do in the months and years to come.

JULIA LOREN

PART 1

PROPHETIC WARNINGS OF DISASTERS TO COME

CHAPTER 1

ONCE IN A BLUE MOON: PROPHETIC WORDS ABOUT NATURAL DISASTERS

by Julia Loren

"If they say the moon is belewe
We must believe that it is true."
—From a 1524 English pamphlet
"Rede Me and Be Not Wrothe"

It was early summer. A family from church—ardent Christians, people of prayer tuned in to the voice of the Holy Spirit—had just sold their house in an upscale neighborhood east of San Diego. The couple had felt the strong prompting of the Lord to move quickly. And so they did. Since they were going out of town to prepare their new house for the imminent move, they asked me to house-sit. I moved in for a couple of weeks and one morning, in the middle of my sojourn in that house, I was startled by an angel.

I stood in the den worshiping the Lord loudly, freely, reveling in the atmosphere of God's presence that seems to reside in houses soaked with prayer. Suddenly, a movement in the hallway startled me. I stepped into the foyer between the den and the living room, hoping that I had not left the front door open to some stranger who decided to waltz right on in. A tall, thin young man, dressed in a white tunic, had not walked through an open door but passed right through it, and kept walking straight into the living room. He turned to look at me as he kept on, never breaking his stride. I dashed into the foyer and turned right into the living room to get a closer look. He passed easily through the wall of the house as if it were smoke. For several long minutes, I stood, amazed, pondering the fact that I actually saw an angel materialize who spoke not a word nor gave a hint as to why he had come. After a while, I sensed that he was walking the neighborhood, marking the territory. For what, I did not know.

A month later, my friends had moved. And I stood on the dock of a marina watching the smoke-filled sky turn the bright Southern California day into a reddish, hellish night at high noon, the ash falling in a thick layer of sooty black upon the deck of my sailboat in Dana Point Marina despite the fires being easily 50 miles away. Later in the week, the moon turned a bluish hue. Red skies. Blue moons. Rare, natural, or man-made disasters that create events of great significance to individuals change the colors of our lives and whole communities.

It seemed apocalyptic, I thought. Scary. Fueled by drought that seemed no worse than other years but different, somehow. The neighborhood where I had been house-sitting burned to the ground that week. My friends, who had heeded the prompting of the Lord to sell and move, got out just in time. I believe the angel I saw while house-sitting was marking the houses of those who were believers and releasing warnings ahead of time.

Years later, in Colorado Springs the summer of 2012, I saw great billowing clouds of smoke edging closer one day, further away the next depending on which way the winds blew. Fueled by drought. Apocalyptic, I thought again. Scary. A new form of super fire, according to the media reports, had firefighters flummoxed as to how to contain it. Eventually, it was contained. But the media reports of super fires fueled by droughts and wind and an increase in highly flammable chemicals falling on the trees from chem-trails released by jets overhead becoming more normal than rare, left me wondering how the rare will become the new normal in the years ahead. What used to happen once in a blue moon is happening more frequently and displacing many more lives as a result.

Blue moons are not that rare. The term *blue moon* is the name for the third full moon in a season that has four full moons, instead of the usual three. The second full moon in one calendar month is also sometimes called a blue moon. The most literal meaning of *blue moon* is when the moon (not necessarily a full moon) appears to a casual observer to be unusually bluish, which is a rare event. The effect can be caused by smoke or dust particles in the atmosphere, as has happened after forest fires in Sweden and Canada in 1950 and 1951, and after the eruption of Krakatoa in 1883, which caused the moon to appear blue for nearly two years. Other less potent volcanoes have also turned the moon blue. People saw blue moons in 1983 after the eruption of the El Chichón volcano in Mexico, and there are reports of blue moons caused by Mount St. Helens in 1980 and Mount Pinatubo in 1991.

When skies turn red and moons turn blue, we cannot help but think that the end is near. Science demystifies the reasons behind the color changes created by fire and wind, but prophets, priests, and the superstitious love to interpret the signs of nature as end-time signs. If priests and prophets say the moon is blue for a reason, who is say that it is not true? If scientists explain the rare events of climate change and natural disasters are now the new normal, who is to say it is not true? Perhaps both interpret correctly the things they "see."

A completely bluish moon may become more common as fires, volcanoes, earthquakes, hurricanes, and tornados make their presence known increasingly around the world. In fact, some believe they are increasing in size and scope and wreaking more costly havoc and damage than ever before. Prophets predict them. Scientists do, too. The chances of a major disaster—man-made or nature-originated—impacting you is no longer as rare as a blue moon. How deeply you are impacted depends on how intently you listen—not to others, but to the voice of the Lord speaking directly to you.

ARE YOU TUNED IN?

I've known many ordinary believers who experienced extraordinary dreams, visions, and angelic visitations that spoke of events about to unfold throughout the nations. Maybe you are one who has heard extraordinary things from heaven—or even in a vision of heaven. Some of the people I know had predictive dreams or visions that were accurate. Others were not. All visions and dreams reveal only partial information that is open to interpretation in many ways.

I once saw a vision of a major school shooting that morphed into a cloud of airborne debris that rolled down city streets terrifying the people who ran ahead of it. I predicted the general area of the school shooting, immediately discerning that it would take place in the school district I was working in that year. But I had no clue that the rest of the vision was about September 11th. I was given no details as to the location, the event, or the date. In fact, I could have interpreted the scene of airborne debris as ash from a volcano, smoke from a fire, or even a nuclear bomb. All I wanted to do was put the image out of my mind—especially after attending to the aftermath of the school shooting at Santana High School that spring.

Years later, in a dream, I received the date December 26 and "saw" that a major disaster would expose much of the child sex slave industry and would be broadcast on Oprah's show for months. The Indonesia and Thailand tsunami occurred on that date and Oprah's show broadcast exactly what I "saw" that she would do in the dream. But I didn't know the exact country or the type of disaster that would happen. I also saw, in another dream, the "royal flush" of leaders out of Arab nations—the "Arab Spring," a few years before it unfolded. But, again, I had no idea of the timing. I only saw in part. As we all do.

No one knows the whole truth about what is about to occur in the future. We hear bits and pieces. And then it takes years to decipher the language of heaven, the ways God speaks to us individually, through dreams, visions, and angelic visitation. Some dreams are more literal while most are simply symbolic. Some visions can be the product of our own imaginations. Some angels that seem like they are from God may be imposters appearing as angels of light—when in fact they are sent from Lucifer's camp. No matter how long we have walked with God, we can still be deceived by our own soul or deceived by the enemy. No one is immune. Everything must be tested and discernment is the key to understanding spiritual experiences.

BLUE MOON PROPHETS

Over the past couple of years, a group of prophets has shifted into talking about futuristic headlines speaking about an earthquake going to happen here or a tornado there, a riot in the streets, food shortages, chaos coming as we move into a new, uncertain era. They are calling us to prepare mentally and in some cases physically. I call this group of prophets the "Blue Moon Prophets" because of the name of the conference that hosts their futuristic ideas.

Prophetic minister and musician Larry Randolph[1] lives outside of Nashville, Tennessee where he hosts an annual prophetic conference called "Blue Moon," holding the first one in 2011 and another Blue Moon event in the fall of 2012 specifically to focus on the coming days. The invited speakers included Terry Bennet, Bob Jones, and John Paul Jackson. Their prophetic predictions unsettled many listeners. But for the most part, those who listened to the Blue Moon prophets agreed on one thing—events that used to happen once in a blue moon are no longer rare. The coming days are getting more frightening, and we need to mobilize to prayer and practical preparation to meet the coming days with faith rather than succumb to fear.

Some might think doom and gloom prophecies are primitive hogwash. "Preppers" (those who focus on preparing for end-time scenarios) gravitate toward them like flies on road kill. But somewhere in the middle lie the curious Christians who seek to find a balance between listening prayerfully and responding respectfully to Blue Moon prophets and prophecies.

The Blue Moon prophets themselves attempt to strike an interesting balance between the Word and the Spirit. During the 2011 conference, Larry spoke about impending earthquakes in places not normally seen. But he is also a believer in the power and authority of the believer to calm the earth and increase damage control:

> This summer the Lord talked to me about seven earthquakes coming, each one up to 7.0 and 8.0 on the Richter scale. Within a few months, we had three or four of those. There are two or three more of those coming. There are some great shakings to come next year and we are going to see them in some very extreme places where we didn't think they would happen. So God is arising to shake terribly the earth, so we need to pray against some of those destructions and that they will be reduced.

Indeed, those disasters may be mitigated by prayer, as well as miracles released during the hurricanes, tornadoes, and earthquakes that were just around the corner.

PACIFIC NORTHWEST—VANCOUVER AND SEATTLE

Prophetic minister Terry Bennett, who used to live in Kansas City but has since moved to the Nashville, Tennessee region, has a track record of amazing encounters with an angel of the Lord who released various dates regarding geo-political events to come. Among them was the prediction of a 9.1 earthquake in Japan that occurred in 2011.

Terry has actually experienced several visions where the angel Gabriel visited him. During one visitation, Gabriel released the headlines of major news stories that would occur between 2011 and 2015.[2]

Among the headline news revealed by Gabriel during a visitation on December 25, 2010 were the following:

- "Canadian Quake Shocks British Columbia—Vancouver Affected"
- "Sleepless in Seattle—Mt. Rainier Awakens While Residents Lose Sleep"
- "The Dark Night of the Soul—Plume Cloud Covers Over Half of the US"

One thing the Lord spoke to him about was an impending earthquake that would shatter the Pacific Northwest from Vancouver, British Columbia to Seattle. Terry had no idea of the fault lines in the region including the Cascadia subduction zone and the Whidbey fault lines—either of which could set off an earthquake that would demolish the entire region. One city collapsing is a major disaster, but two cities at once would overwhelm the region.

Terry also did not know that in 2011, emergency management planners were already collaborating between the two countries to prepare response and recovery plans for just such a scenario. However, what Terry saw and heard was more than an earthquake. In the vision, he stood in Vancouver and looked south where he saw a volcano erupting. In the same time frame, an earthquake and tsunami occurred, as if a triple whammy disaster was unfolding simultaneously.

Something the Lord told me in 1999, when I was standing in California praying about the prophetic words given to many about an impending catastrophic earthquake. The Lord rebuked me and said, "You prophets are always talking about what's going to happen in California, but I want you to understand that the greater fault line is in the Pacific Northwest." He told me that He would release three things—an earthquake, tsunami, and volcano—not just one.

Later, Terry claims that Gabriel visited him again and gave him an actual date for the Vancouver to Seattle devastating quake. That date has passed without incident. But often in the Bible, dates were left misinterpreted or un-interpreted, like Daniel pondering the meaning of "a time, times and half a time," and Jesus saying, "No man will know the hour."

Since I live in the Pacific Northwest and my house is situated on an island located approximately one hour north of Seattle and one hour south of Vancouver, British Columbia, I started researching scientific predictions on an impending quake in the region. What I discovered in August 2011 sent chills down my spine and made me realize that the disastrous prophecies of Terry Bennet may have been averted, but maybe not for long.

Scientists were panicked about a deep tremor (called an "ETS") occurring three months ahead of schedule. This ETS burst on July 23, 2011 right under the Washington State capitol building (perhaps spiritually symbolic) and started moving slowly north. Another one started in early August. Scientists believe that a major earthquake event would be triggered by an ETS.

I immediately purchased earthquake insurance and started praying peace into the earth. I stocked up on a month's supply of food, water, and emergency supplies in case I needed to camp out on my property, and then stashed it in a place easily accessible in case the house totally collapsed. Then, I told neighbors how they could access my cache if they needed it because I was usually out of town. Later, I talked with my community association about getting a hand pump at the site of one of our wells so that we could pump water if a major earthquake demolished the pipes and electricity. Why not be practical? Even the Proverbs 31 woman could laugh at the days to come—because she was prepared. Prepare for what you can, be at peace, forget about it, and enjoy life.

Meanwhile, I alerted my friend and fellow islander, filmmaker Michael Lineau[3] about the ETS, and Michael immediately sent out a prayer alert email explaining the significance of an ETS to many intercessors:

> In my film *Cascadia*, I interviewed a Canadian seismologist about something that he began studying several years ago called ETS—Episodic Tremor and Slip. Every 14-15 months, seismologists have detected a roughly M7 earthquake happening in the Cascadia region, in very slow motion for several weeks as opposed to regular earthquakes where energy is released over seconds or minutes. No one can feel them, but sensitive instruments record them and it has piqued the curiosity of seismologists ever since. They believe that it is during one of these slips that an M9+ megathrust earthquake and tsunami would most likely be triggered!

> Interesting that the tremor "hovered" in Olympia until August 5th. On August 6th we were in Olympia praying with a group of intercessors.

Michael Lineau noted that Washington State has a horrible record of treaty violations and abuse of the Native American tribes and was the first state to legalize abortion, marijuana, and same-sex marriage. As a result, some Christians believe the sin of the state has permeated the land and unleashed both natural and spiritual consequences. The intercessors blended their prayers with repentance and warfare to keep the land from rebelling against the sins of the state.

In addition to that early tremor, a second deep tremor struck the Olympic Peninsula and started moving slowly north during the first week in August. A couple of small earthquakes under 4.0 were felt in the region. As a result, local newspapers started running stories about the scientists' reports and disaster preparedness.

In September 2012, the "Big One" still had not happened along the Cascadia fault line. However, the ETS deep earth tremor once again ran up the coast and set off a M7.7 earthquake in a remote island chain off the north coast of British Columbia. A very small tsunami was recorded in Maui. Again in the spring of 2013, several ETS bursts were recorded along the Cascadia fault line. The only earthquake noted during those bursts was in California. The west coast had dodged the big one for now.

THE POWER OF PRAYER

So what happened to Terry Bennet's word about the great Pacific Northwest earthquake, tsunami, and volcano triple whammy disaster scenario that he says was given to him by the angel Gabriel? Maybe he missed it. Or maybe the disaster was averted through the power of prayer. The prayers of the righteous prevail. The authority we carry as Christians to speak peace into the land is part of our birthright.

Prophetic minister Bob Jones had also predicted a powerful earthquake leveling the Seattle and Vancouver region years ago. Now in his 80s, Bob has been around Charismatic circles for decades.[4] Considered a "parabolic prophet," Bob often speaks in stories or ties his prophetic words to stories. However, he speaks most clearly when uttering predictive prophecies, leaving little to the imagination.

Years ago, Bob Jones talked about a major earthquake that would be coming to Japan. He said that it would set off cataclysmic events and herald the start of economic meltdown around the world. Other prophetic voices concurred. And the earthquake on March 11, 2011 and resulting tsunami happened, to the shock and horror of the world.

Bob also foresaw an M7 quake centered in Northern California but south of San Francisco, reporting that the bridges would be dangerous and that "the world will witness it." It struck during the first game of the World Series that year, October 17, 1989, which was being played in San Francisco, and it was being broadcast to 160 nations who witnessed it live, accurately fulfilling all that Bob had predicted. My father decided to go home from work early that day and drove his customary route across one of the San Francisco bridges that collapsed an hour after he was safely home.

Fortunately, Bob also speaks about judgment averted just as clearly. He believes that the intercessions of the people of the region have since cancelled the earthquake. While speaking at a church near Seattle in 2011, he led the people in prayer and repentance then pronounced the earthquake event averted.

It is interesting to note that Michael Lineau and a group of intercessors found themselves praying in Olympia, Washington during the ETS that, unbeknownst to them at the time, started under their feet and could have triggered a M7-9 earthquake. Olympia, it so happens, is the capitol of Washington State. The focused prayers of the faithful who heed the call to prayer may have caught the ear of God in their repentance and renewed a season of grace and peace into the land. Since the 2012 elections, where Washington State voted to legalize same-sex marriage and cannabis for "recreational use" and profitable sales taxes, intercessors are troubled. Many believe the impact the sin of the land may yet have disastrous effects on the deep fault lines that lay beneath our feet.

The earth could yet slip and quake tomorrow. But prayer warriors still prevail!

CALIFORNIA EARTHQUAKE PROPHECIES

Many prophets also speak about a horribly destructive earthquake demolishing Los Angeles. Here are two prophetic perspectives on what might happen: Rick Joyner of MorningStar Ministries based outside of Charlotte, North Carolina, and Bob Jones both talk about an impending earthquake and believe that Californians should ask God if they should move out of the state.

In a 2011 MorningStar Prophetic Bulletin, Rick Joyner wrote:

> When the major quake hit Kobe, Japan, Bob was sure that was not the one he had seen. When Bob walked into the service last Sunday after the recent 9.0 quake, tsunami, and nuclear meltdown, I immediately asked him if this was the one. I've never seen such concern in Bob's face as he answered, "You know what this means."

What Does It Mean?

> It marks a demarcation point after which great change will come to the whole world, including an ultimate meltdown of the economy. It will also be followed by a major quake on the West Coast of the United States.

> Of course, when and where on the West Coast that this major quake is going to hit are important questions. Bob was not given a timing on this quake but was only told that it would not come before the big one he had been shown in Japan. Now it can come. However, this does not necessarily mean that it is immediate. It could come today, or it could still be years away. We are praying that it still will be delayed, so that everyone who will hear the warning and should move will be able to do this in an orderly way.

> This does not mean that everyone there, even those who may be near ground zero, should move. Some may be called by God to stay and be used during this impending catastrophe. However, until now, we have counseled all who asked if they should leave the West Coast not to do this unless they heard from the Lord to do so. Now we

will begin counseling everyone to leave unless they hear from the Lord to stay.

Not all prophets believe that California will be hit with the "Big One" in their lifetime. To balance the doomsday predictions, Dr. Bill Hamon, founder of Christian International Ministries, and Kim Clement in Hollywood, California reveal the mercy of God who is able to stop it and how we can co-labor with God to transform the region through prayer and blessing.

What are the signs that the Los Angeles earthquake would alter the topography of the state? Bob Jones believes that the tectonic plates are under so much pressure that a volcano will erupt first and the eruption will signal an imminent earthquake along the San Andreas Fault. During the 2011 Blue Moon Conference hosted by Larry Randolph, Bob stated this:

> I believe the next one is getting ready to happen when this volcano erupts when the plates can't take the pressure anymore. And I believe the pressure is melting the plates down there to where this has got to be vented, and these earthquakes are just a sign of what is getting ready to happen. It's getting ready to blow! When it does, it will break loose all the way to the Sea of Cortez, right up the Los Angeles River. And that plate in there will separate from the United States, and you can drive a boat up that river. You can go from the Gulf of Cortez to the Pacific Ocean. And Death Valley will be a great inland sea. And we aren't far from that.

Dr. Bill Hamon believes the opposite. In an article posted on his website titled, "Dr. Bill Hamon's Prophetic Word for California Concerning Impending Earthquake,"[5] he writes that forces may be set in motion but our prayer is more powerful:

> There is a divine principle that God established when he made man upon the earth and gave him dominion over all things concerning earth. "God will do nothing upon the earth without man's participation." Adam and

Eve lost that full authority by their disobedience to God. Jesus came to earth and became God manifest in a human body. Jesus, by obedience even to death on the cross and resurrection from the dead, restored to all mankind in Christ original participation with authority and dominion. That is why the Church can be the determining factor for what happens or doesn't happen on the earth.

The Science Daily News stated in their paper on April 16, 2008: "California has more than a 99% chance of having a magnitude 6.7 or larger earthquake within the next 30 years. The likelihood of a major quake of magnitude 7.5 or greater in the next 30 years is 46%, and such a quake is most likely to occur in the southern half of the state." Only the prayers of the Saints can prevent it from happening.

...God wants Christians to be more kingdom-of-God conscious than earthquake conscious. Pray with faith and reality for God's kingdom to come and His will to be done in California as it is in heaven. God wants to send a manifestation of His glory beyond anything the earth has ever seen. God's declared ultimate purpose is for the earth to be filled with the glory of the Lord as the waters cover the sea (Numbers 14:21; Habakkuk 2:14). The Church needs to pray, preach, and demonstrate the kingdom in faith more than being fearful of earthquakes.

My prophetic admonition to California Christians is for them to take no action based on fear, but only move by divine revelation and faith. Jesus is our only protection and provision regardless of where we are in America or anywhere in the world. I pray for the spirit of wisdom and revelation to rest upon all Christians in California. Amen.

Shawn Bolz and Kim Clement, well-known prophetic ministers who live in California, also believe that God would not "send" an earthquake to California.

Shawn Bolz has heard Bob Jones talk about both an impending earthquake and nuclear fallout impacting Los Angeles. According to an article titled "More Perspective on Earthquakes and Prophecies on the West Coast: The Words of Bob Jones and Rick Joyner" posted by Shawn Bolz on his website, we need to respond carefully to what we hear:

> About the earthquake and nuclear fallout: God has not been speaking to anyone I know in California about this theme for now. No one *in* California or the West Coast is getting these words on a level to suggest to people to actually move away. I am not trying to create a warring perspective between the west coast and east coast prophets but consider this:
>
> Rick Joyner and Bob Jones don't have a deep love for California and think it is a place where too much evil happens. Both of them have had little to no good prophecy for California.
>
> It is the same for me, I am not debunking Rick or Bob but I am judging their words and want to say a few things about them.
>
> 1) These words are not promises from God but they are warnings. Bob Jones gave a warning several years ago about a tsunami in LA hitting in 2010. There was not one, but in the natural we had the state prepare for one and put up tsunami signs. Over 70 believers here that I know began to have dreams about tsunamis and most of them hadn't heard Bob's word. We began to pray and there was statewide prayer organized by several different organizations and the tsunami didn't come. Praise God!

2) Words from God should not cause mass panic and fear but perspective and hope: You can't tell people by the millions to move away without strategy...this is just foolish. If God was really giving us a perspective of mercy to move away because some big devastation was going to happen, then we should have a clearer directive than, "Move away; nuclear power is going to wipe you out, probably in six months." Bob's most recent words were to move away by September 2011. What we can do with this is ask God together on the West Coast for strategy. What *should* we do besides prayer? Maybe nothing, maybe something. When has anything terrible been unavoidable in the whole New Testament?

3) Words from God should carry clear instruction: When Agabus prophesied a drought in Acts, it was so that the believers were ready and could store up enough food (not just for them but for their small region). This drought affected less than 100,000 people and they were completely prepared with strategy and understanding on what to do. The words Bob gave were not clear and had no apostolic preparation. That means that the clearest way to respond is still intercession or moving. Those are the only two choices we were given by him.

4) God always has an army in the hardest places: Those of you who know you are supposed to be here, you are the army of the Kingdom who can help if something terrible does happen. That means you get to do relief and restoration and there is nothing like seeing the Kingdom move when there is so much need! It's amazing. I have done relief for over 20 years off and on, and God just shows up in the most beautiful way. It's a good time to do disaster preparedness and learn what is available in your city.

5) Other prophecies by Bob Jones: One word that Bob gave our friends just last year (and then repeated to us) is that the angel Uriel was standing over the plates in California with one foot on each side and holding them together and as long as the church would keep praying in God's purposes, we would be safe and he would hold them together. I don't know what to do when he just gave that word and is now prophesying about the earthquake but I like the visitation of the angel better then the potential earthquake so we are praying with that.

I am not scared and I don't feel I need to heed their warnings to move except to pray my guts out but I love them. Everyone has to decide for themselves. Again these are not promises from God, they are potentials. We are Christians and we have to exercise power over the storms.

Also I am not rejecting Bob or Rick over my perspective nor am I saying they are wrong. I am just trying to give more perspective so we can be smarter in how we receive their words and what we do about what they are saying. We have to get a lot more intelligent about how we listen.[6]

During a conference held in Anaheim, California on June 25, 2005,[7] prophetic minister Kim Clement predicted a more symbolic earthquake and tsunami. Originally from South Africa, Kim moved his ministry to California a year ago and ministers in a style that the Hollywood set can appreciate—often playing a prophetic piano riff while prophesying. He said:

I want to visit California, and then I want to rest my feet. I wanted to judge the unrighteous and then rest my case, but I heard somebody praying. I heard somebody praying and I stopped. A great tsunami that you don't even know about, says the Spirit. Oh, the desire of the religious to drop this piece of land called California into the sea. But, as I stood before Abraham and he said, "Lord for the sake of just ten," and I found that there were more than ten in California. And I will let you live to see a spiritual tsunami in this state called California. California, you shall live!

While Kim prophesied that a major earthquake would not disrupt California to the extent that other prophets like Bob Jones and Rick Joyner have prophesied for years, he went on to predict a volcanic eruption—again symbolic but also likely in the natural. He prophesied on March 25, 2011 from Nashville, Tennessee:

> "Watch the mountains," says the Lord, "Watch the mountains as they begin to erupt. You see, the earth is busy—from deep within; it has erupted from within. Now it's going to go to the mountains," says the Lord. "There will be minimal loss of lives, but the earth erupting represents an eruption of the Spirit of the Living God upon the nations of the earth!"

> The Lord says, "Watch the mountains! They will erupt and smoke shall come from them, and the people will say, 'Oh my God, it is the end!'" But God said, "It is the beginning, it is the beginning of labor pains, for something is about to be born. An eruption of My Spirit as never before, and I shall bring forth something that will reach every nation on the earth," says the Lord.[8]

THE MISSISSIPPI-JERUSALEM CONNECTION

In addition to predicting the California earthquake, Bob Jones believed one would strike Washington DC in the near future. (One did hit Washington DC in the summer of 2011.) However, the potential for larger impact beyond the Capitol and tied to the Capitol may be completely preventable. Bob predicts that the New Madrid fault line in the Midwest will shift dramatically in the future if the US government shifts its alliance with Israel.

During a conference called "Eyes and Ears" hosted by Jeff Jansen in May 2011, Bob said:

> If NATO troops are used to divide Jerusalem, and the US is a large part of NATO troops, it will be the last thing we do as a nation. The New Madrid Fault Line will divide if we divide Jerusalem. We need to pray for Jerusalem continually. There are plans to invade Israel and divide it. The Church can stop these plans. The church should be praying for Israel continually. You don't really want to know what will happen if we divide Jerusalem. The Mississippi River will cut 35 miles wide. Five of our greatest cities will be gone. This is a warning. Our nuclear plants will melt down there. And this nation will become a third-rate power, a bankrupt nation. If this happens, we will be debt-slaves to other nations and our food supplies will be sent to other nations.
>
> Jerusalem is His footstool. If you check history, every time we've touched anything dealing with Israel, we get hit immediately. Hurricane Katrina was no accident. We gave Gaza away and we got Katrina. You check back every time there is a financial collapse, we had butted into Israel's business. That arrogance and that pride, if we seek to divide Jerusalem in half, everything along the Mississippi River will be gone. The great lakes will break through to the Mississippi and run down to the Gulf.
>
> Keep your hands off of Israel.

According to Bob, if you touch the apple of God's eye, God won't be happy and spiritual forces will be unleashed in the earth—as it is in heaven. God blesses those who bless Israel. Perhaps a generation yet alive on earth will see this major earthquake rip our nation in half. Our political and personal agendas do ripple through the atmosphere, impacting others for generations to come.

FUTURE DROUGHTS AND FAMINES

On several occasions, prophetic minister John Paul Jackson, who also spoke at the 2012 Blue Moon Conference hosted by Larry Randolph, has prophesied about food and water shortages, civil unrest on a massive scale impacting cities, increasing unemployment, and political and economic depression. During an interview with Sid Roth,[9] he revealed that some of John Paul's predictions have come true. One ominous and vague reference echoes in my mind clearly from time to time. After an angelic visitation where many future events were revealed to John Paul, he said this, "I kept hearing an angel saying in a deep, loud voice, 'The woes of 2012. The woes of 2012. The woes of 2012.' I don't know what those woes are. The angel did not tell me about those woes."

There didn't seem to be any major "woes" revealed during 2012—except for the ongoing drama of the United States presidential election revealing a deeply divided American public, the further erosion of individual rights, the ongoing deadly chaos in most of a increasingly destabilized Middle East, continued wars and droughts and famines throughout the world, the economic tremors and austerity measures sending Europe into a panic, and Hurricane Sandy pummeling the East Coast of the United States and the back-to-the-futuristic sinking of the replica HMS Bounty (turned Jack Sparrow's *Pirates of the Caribbean* ship) offshore. Other than that, 2012 seemed pretty routine in the order of inevitable annual incidents of worldwide chaos. Perhaps the "woes" were set up during 2012 and have yet to reveal the full impact. Every year has its "woes." Either they are becoming more frequent and impacting more people, or our global internet media has transformed us into a very small global village where we are all instantly aware of what is happening to each other.

Although John Paul Jackson didn't identify specific woes of 2012, apparently the angels who spoke to him and released news headlines in visions scattered across years told him plenty about woes beyond 2012 that include droughts, famine, food shortages, civil unrest, riots on the streets of the US, and economic meltdown that is yet to become as severe as foreseen.

One of the things he saw was a coming drought when water would become a huge issue. We know that this is a huge issue in African countries and nations around the world. However, he believes that at some point in the future, city tap water in the US will be more expensive than oil.

> We're talking about water that's normally fairly inexpensive becoming very expensive. In fact, various cities in the United States would have to evacuate thousands of people because there wouldn't be enough water in the reservoirs, and in the aquifers that they get the water from, to get water to all the people.

Along with the water shortage would be a food shortage— but not necessarily tied in to drought conditions.

> I saw a blight coming to hybrid seeds, and that would bring a type of famine to the United States. So the hybrid seeds that have been propagated by various corporations, supposedly resistant to all kinds of things, will actually allow for a blight to come. Some of the seeds won't break the ground. Some of the seeds will break the ground but never bear fruit, and so you'll end up seeing green out in the fields. There will be enough rain for them in certain areas, but they won't come to seed. So there won't be the corn that would normally be in the ear. There won't be the wheat that is normally in the head of wheat. So that creates a major food shortage.

Droughts, fights over food, riots in the street, and a lack of drinking water have all been realities in the past decade but are projected to become worse. It seems as if we are in for 50 years of hot summers, dwindling water supplies or deluges of rain, persistent droughts and huge populations of people shifting out of climate-ravaged areas and on the road for their nearest neighbors, overwhelming infrastructures and possibly leading to an increase in global genocides.

But that is the plan of the antichrist spirit on the loose to rob, kill, and destroy. God's plan is to redeem all of creation—leading to a new you and a new earth. How that gets accomplished is a mystery beyond my revelation.

Although John Paul Jackson and the Blue Moon prophets have seen headlines of the future in their visions, many scientists have seen those same headlines as they document climate changes that are occurring most evidently since 2008 and will continue for the next couple of decades. The Blue Moon Prophets may just be seeing what is ahead if we do not repent, turn from our dependence on fossil fuels and our self-focused materialism, and change our ways.

Many scientists have been calling for a reduction in the use of fossil fuels that they believe create global warming and result in dramatic climate disruptions. It seems as if they are paving the way for a global action plan of "repentance" that also needs to start with individuals and grass roots changing their thoughts and ways in order to influence politicians to amend their ways.

ADAPTING TO FUTURE EVENTS[10]

According to journalist and author Mark Hertsgaard, climate change and global warming are largely to blame for the increase and destructive potential in super storms around the world. His extensive interviews through the years with international scientists reveal a global scenario that is truly frightening. He documents them in his book *Hot: Living Through the Next Fifty Years on Earth.*

In short, global scientists say that we are too late. Over the next 50 years, while populations explode, climate change will transform our world in ways we never imagined. How we grow our food, construct our buildings, organize economies, control borders, and help our children plan for the future will be very different from the past.

Military experts call climate change a "threat multiplier." It will worsen existing conflicts over water supplies, energy sources, and migration caused by climate refugees. Economic prosperity is being challenged. Approximately 25 percent of the US gross national product is at risk from extreme weather events.

Super storms and massive flooding in various regions of the world coupled with droughts are sure to increase the number of climate "refugees" around the world who are crossing borders due not just to war, but because their homes and villages are literally underwater. The world must begin to plan for adaption to environmental changes. Reversing the path of global warming will take time, and in the meanwhile disasters of unprecedented magnitude will continue to happen. You may be able to control the climate in your house with the flip of a switch, or turn of a dial, or press of a button, but the world is a much bigger "house" to transform.

According to Mark, what international scientists believe could happen in the days ahead includes:

- Polar ice melts increase the sea level, resulting in low-lying coastal areas being permanently flooded. Bangladesh would cease to exist, pushing climate refugees into India; New York would be under water, as well as Venice, Italy; your local airport, if built at sea level by or on a body of water (San Francisco, Oakland, Washington D.C.) would also be under water; you cannot build sea walls every-where so neighborhoods wiped out by a storm may have to be replaced by wetlands—barriers to future storms. There will be losses. Perhaps your house will be lost, or even your country.

- The Gulf Stream would shift and Europeans would find themselves battling constant cold.
- Persistent droughts like the one in Darfur would cause climate refugees to try to cross into other countries and border wars would break out; the new housing developments in many nations would look like refugee camps.
- Wildfires will spread rapidly and out of control in many nations.
- Water supplies will dwindle.
- The rich may turn up their air conditioning or crank up their heaters, but the poor and elderly do not have a chance to survive or thrive.

Despite his gloomy outlook, Mark sees hope. Communities and countries are waking up to the fact that they have to plan to mitigate against future disasters and beef up their infrastructure. We are learning from such super storms as Hurricane Katrina in 2005 and Hurricane Sandy in 2012, from the wildfires in Colorado of 2012, and the tsunami in Japan in 2011. And we are realizing that we have to adapt to an increase in such events before we can change the way we live and reverse the impact of climate change.

Between 2007 and 2009, US green gas emissions declined by 9 percent. Largely due to the economic recession, businesses reducing their carbon footprint and increasing their use of alternative energy (green) launched a journey to more sustainable living. Leading nations are "repenting"—turning from the way they are doing things. G8 leaders are agreeing to limit green gas emissions and seek more sustainable energy treaties.

Smaller communities are also leading us back into an old/new way of adapting to economic and climate changes. Many are creating their own economies to develop bartering and local food growth campaigns as economic woes continue to plague the European countries and the US. Families of the future may just grow more food and spend less, their houses completely solar and wind powered; cars will be running on fuel sources completely independent of oil.

So we have prophets talking about what the world is going to look like and scientists agreeing with their "visions." So far we have talked about the earth. But the heavens are also a concern.

SOLAR DISTURBANCES AND POLAR SHIFTS

Terry Bennett and other prophets also saw solar disturbances coming, beginning in 2012, that would seem apocalyptic and dramatic, frightening in their impact on earth. According to Terry's word given during a conference in Kansas City in spring of 2011, solar disturbances would alter life as we know it.

He believes that the sun's rising and setting would be altered throughout the earth as the earth tilted and time zones changed. Weather patterns would become unpredictable and hurricane seasons would be so altered that hurricanes would start coming at times totally out of season. The gravitational pull surrounding the earth would increase and satellites will be yanked right out of the sky.

Actually, the sun caused other planets within our solar system to act up. They aligned, I don't know how to explain this, I am not a scientist, but they aligned in a funny pattern. It was not a straight line. They aligned themselves in a funny pattern and when they did that, they also affected the earth. But in comparison it was 95% solar as the sun did what it did and brought rolling blackouts, electrical disruption, water distribution disruption because it is run by machinery. It was major throughout the earth.

I saw then, the sun did this weird, funny thing. I do not even know how to describe it but its effect on the earth was incredible. It was like a storm with flares and all of that and the gravitational pull of the earth increased. The magnetism of the earth increased. The tilt of the earth was altered so that time itself changed all over the earth. The satellites were both blinded and some of them were yanked right out of the sky. He blinded the communications of the earth. Cell phones, all types of things, military hardware, commercial hardware, people were blinded, GPS was useless, the magnetic north itself altered which affected all forms of travel especially by sea and by land. They used to be guided by the North Star but the North Star will not be in the same position so it altered...[a polar shift]. It was dramatic.

Everything that deals with waves, sound waves and that type of thing was dramatically affected. Types of equipment, such as pacemakers, were disrupted. A lot of machinery in hospitals was not reliable or it was useless to them. I could see that in airports, in military installations.

SCIENTISTS COMMENT ON POLAR SHIFTS AND SOLAR STORMS

Taking a look at the science behind solar storms and polar shifts predicted by those who interpret psychics and mysterious historical calendars can help us put celestial matters in perspective. NASA's website actually devoted a FAQ page to handle all the questions surrounding 2012 and the "impending doom" from outer space predicted by New Age writers. While NASA representatives comment on asteroids, they do not mention here that an asteroid is indeed scheduled to hit earth—but not until the year

2182. According to scientists, with an estimated probability of 0.07 percent, Apollo asteroid 1999 RQ36 could hit the Earth.

Official NASA comments about the coming years should bring peace to those who feel unsettled. However, scientists did not create the world; they only seek to understand it. Only one Being created the world. And His ways are unfathomable.

2012: BEGINNING OF THE END OR WHY THE WORLD WON'T END?[11]

Q: Is there a planet or brown dwarf called Nibiru or Planet X or Eris that is approaching the Earth and threatening our planet with widespread destruction?

A: Nibiru and other stories about wayward planets are an Internet hoax. There is no factual basis for these claims. If Nibiru or Planet X were real and headed for an encounter with the Earth in 2012, astronomers would have been tracking it for at least the past decade, and it would be visible by now to the naked eye. Obviously, it does not exist. Eris is real, but it is a dwarf planet similar to Pluto that will remain in the outer solar system; the closest it can come to Earth is about 4 billion miles.

Q: What is the polar shift theory? Is it true that the earth's crust does a 180-degree rotation around the core in a matter of days if not hours?

A: A reversal in the rotation of Earth is impossible. There are slow movements of the continents (for example Antarctica was near the equator hundreds of millions of years ago), but that is irrelevant to claims of reversal of the rotational poles. However, many of the disaster websites pull a bait-and-shift to fool people. They claim a relationship between the rotation and the magnetic polarity of Earth, which does change irregularly, with a magnetic reversal taking place every 400,000 years on average. As far as we know, such a magnetic reversal doesn't cause any harm to life on Earth. A magnetic reversal is very unlikely to happen in the next few millennia, anyway.

Q: Is there a danger from giant solar storms predicted for 2012 [or beyond]?

A: Solar activity has a regular cycle, with peaks approximately every 11 years. Near these activity peaks, solar flares can cause some interruption of satellite communications, although engineers are learning how to build electronics that are protected against most solar storms. But there is no special risk associated with 2012. The next solar maximum will occur in the 2012-2014 time frame and is predicted to be an average solar cycle, no different than previous cycles throughout history.

SO WHAT DO WE DO?

Science and prophecy sometimes merge and sometimes diverge. No one really knows exactly how the galaxy works and interacts with the earth and its atmosphere, or how the earth responds to natural and spiritual events. Mystics and scientists disagree often about events to come. Scientists can confirm events and mystics often interpret events according to their spiritual understanding and imagination—in the aftermath. However, prophets have often been right in their predictions, as scientists have been in theirs. No matter what you choose to believe, there is one who knows the beginning from the end—the Creator. And He is worth knowing. You access Him by faith, simply by asking God to reveal Himself to you, to open the eyes of your understanding to know Jesus. God will lead you to Himself and into the truth...if you really want to seek the Truth. *Those who seek Him will find Him.*

It doesn't take a prophetic word to know that the earth is alive and vibrant and natural disasters will happen. Find the purpose of God in your life and seek Him for how you are to respond. Perhaps you are called to help. Perhaps you are called to pray. All of us are clearly being called to prepare spiritually and mentally for the days to come. How big is Christ in you? Is He the hope of glory to you—and can He be so big in you that you will have the mental and spiritual wherewithal to release His glory to others in a day of need? We Christians should be able to rise and shine during a needful and darkened time.

Notes

1. See www.larryrandolph.com.

2. See Terry's website for a list of "headline news": http://www.terrybennett.net/.

3. Michael Lineau has produced PBS documentaries on the region's volcanoes, earthquakes, and disaster preparation for families and businesses, available at http://www.globalnetproductions.com.

4. See http://www.bobjones.org/.

5. See "Dr. Bill Hamon's Prophetic Word for California Concerning Impending Earthquake," http://www.christianinternational.com/index.php?option=com_zoo&task=item&item_id=2711&Itemid=33.

6. Shawn Boltz, "More Perspective on Earthquakes and Prophecies on the West Coast: The Words of Bob Jones and Rick Joyner," Wordpress, April 7, 2011, accessed August 05, 2013, http://shawnbolz.wordpress.com/2011/04/07/more-perspective-on-earthquakes-and-prophecies-on-west-coast-the-words-of-bob-jones-rick-joyner.

7. See http://kimclementvault.com/prophecyread.asp?num=183&keyword=california.

8. See http://kimclementvault.com/prophecyread .asp?num=453&keyword=mountains.

9. See http://www.sidroth.org/site/News2?page=NewsArticle&id =8629&news_iv_ctrl=0&abbr=tv.

10. Mark Hertsgaard, *Hot: Living Through the Next Fifty Years on Earth* (Boston: Houghton Mifflin Harcourt, 2011).

11. These questions and answers are taken from Brian Dunbar, "Beyond 2012: Why the World Didn't End," NASA, December 22, 2012, accessed August 05, 2013, http://www .nasa.gov/topics/earth/features/2012.html.

Chapter 2

DISASTER! THIRTY DAYS AND COUNTING

by Julia Loren

Apparently, after a storm, birds sing.

But I cannot hear them.

Today, I feel oblivious to the fact that birds sing and the sky is blue and in some parts of the world, all is well. All I know is that 30 days after the storm, hell is more real than heaven to those who have been displaced by Hurricane Katrina. And if Katrina is what we can expect to see in the aftermath of disasters in the US, we had best be prepared.

All I know today is that if you can get past the police cruiser blocking off the street along River Road in downtown Baton Rouge, you will easily find a place to park outside the convention center exhibition hall. In fact, you can park anywhere. Despite a heavy police presence, you can park in the middle of the street within the wide center divider if you want to. Forget about the three-hour parking rule in designated parking spots along the side of the street as well. No one will ticket you or tow your car. If you can make it into that part of the city, through the overwhelming traffic and the roadblocks, you can stay as long as you want to. Some rules, in a national disaster, just don't apply.

As I drive down the road seeking a place to park, I notice teenagers and older adults wandering aimlessly outside the Baton

Rouge exhibition hall. A few trudge up the short hill of the levy alongside the Mississippi River, to sit on benches and dream of the river carrying them away from their nightmare existence. One lone boy leans forward on a bench overlooking the river, his head in his hands, perhaps crying, maybe angry, certainly over-whelmed. Life as he knew it drowned in the floodwaters of New Orleans's levy breach and he feels the sea of humanity reaching out its ugly hand to take him down as well. I say a silent prayer for him, wishing I could sit beside him, stretch my arm across his shoulder and tell the boy that it will be all right. But I am not so sure that it will be for him. It will not be all right. Not today. Not tomorrow or for God only knows how long.

Local police officers sit cozily in their cars, engines running, the air conditioning flowing, watching the traffic trickle through while National Guardsmen armed with M-16s walk the streets, keeping a wary eye on individuals and small crowds. The mil-itary presence reminds me that while New Orleans is the war zone, the center of destruction, Baton Rouge is its refugee center. If this were San Francisco after a massive earthquake, San Jose or Sacramento would be the refugee center. If it were Seattle, refugees would flock to Bellevue on the east side, or someplace nearby with a functioning infrastructure. Thousands of people would take to the road looking for food and shelter.

The refugees are predominantly black, primarily from dis-tricts and parishes of New Orleans and South Louisiana that have been flooded beyond hope of recognition. White refugees have families far away and resources to travel. Not so for the poor, the sick, and the elderly. Their homes lie in piles of rubble sur-rounded by a cesspool of mold, oil, and sewage. Many of them, renters to begin with, have no place to go. And so they call the convention center home. And all two garbage bags full of belong-ings now rest near their cots. Someone has to watch for looters or they will take matters into their own hands and life inside the shelters all across Louisiana will get ugly. And so soldiers patrol inside the center as well as outside.

It's been a month since Hurricane Katrina blew away communities and stretched out her hand to crumble the levy's edges, ensuring a flood imagined in the minds of engineers during disaster scenarios yet shrouded in denial as to the possibility. The possibility became inevitable. As a result, hundreds of thousands of families find themselves displaced. Some have been absorbed into other states finding communities willing to sponsor their relocation process. Usually, shelters close within a week or two after a major disaster as people find other places to go. In Louisiana, shelters have been full all month. Many of the almost 500,000 people displaced along the Gulf Coast have discovered that there is no place to go.

INSIDE THE SHELTER AND RECOVERY CENTER

Inside the exhibition hall of the convention center, cots lie in neat rows of about 50 beds in each, row upon row upon row upon row in the cavernous building. More than 1,500 men, women, and children sleep in this cavernous room at night or lounge on these cots during the heat of the day. Blankets fall unto the floor. An old man pulls his around him, closes his eyes as he leans back onto the bed, drawing up his arm to place it over his eyes as if he doesn't want to see what's happening around him. Scarcely 20 feet away from his bed, a makeshift kitchen alongside the wall serves sandwiches and cold drinks to a steady stream of people. National guardsmen in their camouflaged uniforms keep their hands on their rifles, frequently scanning the rows of beds, taking their jobs seriously of protecting not just life but what little property is left to individuals.

Across the street from the shelter, FEMA and state agencies have set up a joint Disaster Recovery Center (DRC). A multi-cultural line forms around the outside of the building from 6 a.m. to 6 p.m. These are the ones who have found shelter elsewhere but had to make their way back to the DRC for further assistance.

Predominately black folks, a few white couples, an East Indian, an occasional person of Asian descent, join the line.

Inside the DRC and outside, whoever is talking dispenses more words than promises—no cash, no immediate, practical help. Inside, state welfare agencies should be handing out food stamps and getting people initial disaster unemployment checks. The white-shirted Red Cross should be handing out hotel vouchers, emergency funds, food vouchers, and other assistance. But the telltale white and red shirts are nowhere in sight. No one knows where all the Red Cross personnel have vanished. Somewhere in New Orleans or Texas or Mississippi perhaps—certainly not here where the largest concentration of people gather seeking help of any kind.

The red shirts are here—representatives from the Army Corp of Engineers, whose mission is to assist homeowners with Operation Blue Roof. They'll send a team out within a week to unroll some blue plastic sheeting and hammer it up to keep the rain and mold away until homeowners' insurance checks are released and contractors are available to complete a proper roof. It's a free temporary fix. Unfortunately, people expect the Army Corp to fix their roof, not patch it. People also expect the federal government to fix their lives, not patch them.

FROM SHOCK TO ANGER

It has been one month since the storm. People are transitioning from shock and denial to anger now. The whole nation seems angry and all the talking heads on television fuel their anger with stories of incompetency.

It's a natural, proven fact that in the aftermath of any disaster heads will roll. Any head will do. Primitive thinking requires a blood sacrifice to appease the angry gods who called down nature's wrath. The one with the greatest visibility promises the greatest relief. So FEMA's director finds his head neatly placed under the executioner's ax. The ax gets raised, diverting people's attention from their woes for a short while. The ax comes down—a clean slice. But the people aren't satisfied. Their attention has just been drawn to a whole agency now set up as the scapegoat—FEMA, the big, bad wolf. FEMA, the reason why I am here.

I am stationed at the Baton Rouge DRC to handle media for FEMA, as a Disaster Assistance Employee working as a field Public Information Officer, another lamb thrown to the wolves. I was called in to replace a woman on the verge of emotional collapse who is going home for a couple of weeks. She may not return.

I took this job because, after several visions and dreams about previous school shootings and the 9/11 twin towers falling, I had been called to assist in the aftermath of the disasters. As a result, I sensed that God wanted me to use all of my education, skills, and talents to obtain the necessary credentials to be on the spot in the aftermath of future disasters. And so, I got on the disaster cadre with FEMA.

I find a place to park outside of the Civic Center area and walk to the DRC. The stench of an overloaded sewage system mixed with a street wash of bleach greets me as I walk past the Sheraton on my way into my office located inside the DRC. Strange brew. The Sheraton houses mainly evacuees and a few workers are lucky enough to get a bed. I was not lucky. My bed is in an old, moldy-smelling cottage located far outside the city near Lafayette. It was the only place I could find. As I walk through the stench on the street, I am glad for the bed that I have.

Walking through the doors, a man wearing a black shirt stops me, his loose-fitting fatigue-like pants and combat boots hang from his perfectly toned body, a pistol evident against his hip. *Is he military or what?* I wonder. He asks for my FEMA badge and lets me through. I ask who he is with and he replies, "Blackwater Security." It is the outfit that the government contracted with to provide security for every federal disaster recovery office. They are everywhere. While not dressed in a uniform, each Blackwater man has the distinct bearing of being a highly trained military man in civilian clothes. Even the way they stand commands respect.

CNN calls on the landline as soon as I step into the near-empty office that holds only an old wooden desk with a stack of papers, official talking points, media desk information and list of phone numbers, a phone, and a chair. For a moment I ponder the possibility of sleeping here tonight, but there is a notice posted on the door: No employees are to sleep in their offices. It is just not safe. The CNN producer has a string of questions, but I only hear one and reply, "No, I won't give you a live interview. I've just gotten in today and am not up to speed on current challenges and the official talking points on various issues." So I redirect them. I find that redirecting them works well. It becomes the FEMA way in this disaster—redirect, deflect, get-the-hell-away-from-me policies work. Local television and print reporters contact me throughout the day, occasionally by phone but often just showing up.

I'm not going on camera. I have no answers.

I wander outside my office and notice a sign that says something about counseling. In the aftermath of most large disasters, FEMA immediately passes along a chunk of money to the state department of mental health, tasking them with hiring trauma counselors who would be in residence in the DRC in case anyone needed them. These counselors are from some American volunteer group. I ask them about their credentials. They have none. One has taken a class in crisis counseling. None hold any advanced degree focusing on counseling—or any degree for that matter. No experience whatsoever. It showed.

So the state used the money to pay volunteers who work for free? Ah...normal government business in these parts. Volunteers are cheap labor. That means more money can be diverted to some other coffer. The volunteers sip coffee and eat donuts. No one wants to talk with them. When an unfortunate traumatized woman is led past the open door of my office to the counseling area in tears, she goes into a room for an extraordinarily short time. I notice her leave as soon as possible. Although I am working here in the capacity of external affairs, I am also a marriage and family therapist and her leaving saddens me. I see the depth of her need and federally financed, inappropriately trained counselors seems inexcusable when legions of trained counselors abound ready and waiting.

POLITICIANS AND VULTURES

But I put her out of my mind as I venture over to the Baton Rouge Capitol Building for a briefing with the mayor of New Orleans and legislature regarding the staged reentry of business owners and homeowners in various districts of New Orleans. Louisiana has a reputation of being the most politically corrupt and one of the most poverty-stricken states in the union. One of the cameramen from a local television station promises to fill me in later—off the job. I can't wait.

During the long wait, big-time, portly local attorneys slap each other on the back, posturing for their piece of the federal money pie, the scent of baking pie driving them wild. They smell class action suits, contracts for their buddies, larger houses, and vacation homes for themselves. And if they manage to sidestep federal prison or heart failure in the years to come, they smell the scent of an early retirement. One of them looks my way and asks who I work for. I tell him that it is confidential. He winks at me, smiles, and looks back at the gathering crowd.

A local senator's aide stands in line outside the DRC when I arrive this morning. He is filing for assistance on a "constituent's" behalf. In the process, he stirs up the crowd yelling out, "If FEMA won't help you, Senator L. will!" and hands out his card with the office phone number. Hands reach out from the crowd eagerly taking his card. The crowd riles easily and their inner heat combines with the heat of the day, threatening to erupt into something ugly.

PEACEKEEPERS—ARMED WITH GUNS AND SANDWICHES

The guards from Blackwater Security, a company in North Carolina that FEMA contracts with, are fantastic. Most are ex-military. While their side arms are visible, the big guns are hidden away with other guards standing by the rear exits of the building. All of them seem to handle the crowd with unceasing patience. They are able to swiftly ease an individual whose mood threatens to escalate beyond reason. Quick to spot a mentally ill person, they handle him with great dignity and repeat their explanations or directions to him patiently until the man seems to understand and walks away. They seem to be really well trained. I've never seen anything like them. The DRC couldn't function without them at the doors, answering preliminary questions and directing the incessant flow of humanity. They calm the crowd by their patience. They command their respect by the evident sidearm and air of authority, an authority the local police do not seem to possess. They make me feel safer for standing near my door.

Blackwater men finesse the crowd to a grumbling quiet and my phone continues to ring as the media calls in their requests and so I continue my job of deflecting and ducking.

The line outside today gets rough with attitudes flaring in the morning as someone, probably from Senator L's office, has organized a protest. Some carry signs with anti-government sentiments. They rail against FEMA as an entity but take care to treat the individual FEMA employees with respect. The line of protesters parts as I walk through them toward my office. I appreciate that, smile; they know we do what we can for them even though we cannot do much.

A volunteer group from the Vineyard Christian Fellowship comes by with sandwiches and soft drinks and water for people in line. Within an hour, the morale outside undergoes a remark-able shift. Someone cares. Someone is offering something more than words. The food raises their faith, if not in God's caring pres-ence, in hope that something more substantial will come through today—like manna from heaven. Peace subdues the crowd. I call the church and ask them to please come back tomorrow. I tell the woman on the phone that the sandwiches really boosted morale but don't mention how nasty the crowd was before they arrived. I don't want to scare them. The afternoon passes more easily.

Later in the day, I hear the nerve-wracking sound of metal on metal and the crowd outside my window erupts with cheers and clapping. I wander outside to see what wondrous event has bro-ken the monotony and entertains the crowd. On my way to the door someone asks, "Is that your car? A grey Ford Focus?" I nod. An eighteen-wheeler has kissed my rear. The bumper hangs like a lopsided, wicked grin. The driver is young, black, looking very, very worried. I glance back at the crowd of blacks sweltering in line outside the door, waiting for FEMA assistance. They are all staring at me, quiet now, tensing up, anticipating a second act to the show—an angry tirade by a white woman perhaps.

I know that how I handle this could touch off a riot among the agitated crowd. I start laughing and my audience relaxes, laughs, and continues to watch while I introduce myself to the driver and say, "Hey, no worries. It's just a rental car." He tells me that he is afraid to lose his job and he has a young family to support. I nod, and then walk back inside for my license and bottles of cold water for the driver and the cops attending to the scene.

Technically, it's his fault, the officers say. "Technically, I am illegally parked so it is my fault," I gently remind the officers. "In the midst of the vast sea of pressing human needs, a mangled bumper on a rental car is of no real consequence." The cops agree. Neither of us is cited. We chat with his supervisors who have arrived on the scene and I tell them that the cops said I could park illegally and because of the obstruction the driver and I would not be cited. The cops confirm this and the young man lightens up when his supervisors say it won't affect his job. The crowd sees the relief flooding his face and, show over, they return to their own conversations.

I've been here three days and can't wait to get home. Three days of the reek of sewage drifting up from the hot asphalt, the endless parade of faces blank with despair or weighted down by grief and anger, the misinformation, the military presence and imposed martial law, the lack of answers and most objectionably, the complete failure to get this population resettled into a more dignified living state.

I drive back to my moldy Cajun County cottage near Lafayette, 55 minutes outside Baton Rouge that evening, bumper flapping in the breeze, listening to the 6:15 conference call on my way. I am amazed that I am leaving work so early. Those who work inside the public affairs office are working 12 to 15 hours a day, six or seven days a week. Since I am working in the field, I fall more under the rules of curfew. The boss doesn't want me or other FEMA employees out after dark. In fact, by day I am to keep the FEMA badge that swings from my neck completely out of sight unless I am asked for it while trying to enter a building.

I am lucky to find this place to sleep. Other workers are sleeping in their cars, or on the army barge tied up to the bank of the river across from the Civic Center, or tripled up in hotel rooms, or trying to sleep in the dorm at the joint field office. All the public information officers in the field are sleeping where they can as well. At present, they are on the phone talking about pressing issues in New Orleans, or specific media or individuals who raise questions that we have no answers to. Those in the field who have worked for FEMA the longest have a distinct edginess to their voices. They have internalized the frustrations of the masses as well as their own powerlessness. The media questions are predictable. Veteran field PIOs however, stand amazed that our answers are no longer predictable.

I arrive at my cottage just as the conference call ends. This day was difficult. It started with a migraine that lingered throughout the day and ended with the sounds of my frustrated co-workers ringing in my ears. I think of drinking a soda and eating the burger I had just picked up. But it's seven o'clock and it's still light outside and I am not really hungry. I opt for a jog instead to run it out of my system. I pound out the answerless questions, the sights and sounds of the masses, the floppy bumper. I rush past the thick-bodied steer chewing on a bale of hay, past the sugar cane field bent by the winds and rendered practically unharvestable by the recent hurricanes, and slow to a light jog past a family lounging in their front yard, a normal family, descendents of Cajuns who have lived on the land for years and will live there for years to come. It is nice to see a normal family lounging together in the safety of their own yard. I know I'll sleep better for it.

CHURCHES AS CITIES OF REFUGE

Churches everywhere are housing refugees. The government cannot do the job, but the communities can and they do so quickly. Unencumbered by politics and MOUs, they go to work, opening hearts, homes, and church buildings in the immediate aftermath of the hurricane. More than a month later, they are still at work. I cannot image where all these refugees would have gone if no churches existed. They would likely be living in tents along the side of the road, starving, one month after the disaster. Southerners, both white and black, throughout Louisiana and Mississippi seem to have put aside any sense of overt or covert racism and stepped up to a sense of duty. As one man stated, "We are just doing our Christian duty, ma'am." But duty seems to be an acquisition of a more recent value system in the South. In the past, racism and economic self-interest dictated how men and women would respond to disaster victims. Certainly not in this day and age would we dare to repeat the past. Or have we already?

In 1927, the great Mississippi flood demolished miles of farmland in the states it flowed through, with Arkansas being hit the hardest. During the disaster, 700,000 people were displaced, including 330,000 African-Americans who were moved to 154 relief camps. Over 13,000 evacuees near Greenville, Mississippi, were gathered from area farms and evacuated to the crest of an unbroken levee, and stranded there for days without food or clean water, while boats arrived to evacuate white women and children. Many blacks were detained and forced to labor at gunpoint during flood relief efforts. The only difference between then and now is that we are not forcing blacks at gunpoint to get to work in relief efforts. Now we let them sit under the watchful eye of men with guns, encouraging them to do nothing. No one offers them a job clearing debris. No one knows what to do with the refugees so, one month after the storm, there they sit like wind-blown branches fallen from trees.

If the church members haven't suffered some loss, they are helping someone who has. The sandwich people from the Vineyard return to the DRC. I liked them immensely, so much so that I decide to go home with them. Tina and George, a church-affiliated couple, invite me to use their guest room rather than make the long drive to Lafayette. There are still no hotel rooms available. There are if you have something to bargain with, but I don't feel like bargaining and a home appeals much more than a hotel. Sunday, I take the day off and attend church with them. I am exhausted. From the looks of everyone in that church service, they are, too.

Something about a good music set lowers emotional defenses and purges the soul. During this morning's service at the Vineyard Baton Rouge, I try not to dissolve in tears as a flood of images of human suffering parades before my mind's eye. I let each image rise up and march out of my consciousness. As I struggle against my emotions, I remember that it's OK to weep with those who weep—but no one is weeping in here. Some in the congregation are evacuees who lost everything and are now housed in a relative's home nearby. But they're not weeping. So I hold back. It's a largely tearless but a necessary purge that happens sweetly in this building full of a peaceful presence. I leave all the images there, hanging in the air of the church building, in the atmosphere of God where all the sights and sounds and smells and people can find a resting place in Him.

Pete Kennedy, the Vineyard Baton Rouge pastor, is spearheading major relief efforts and coordinating donations and volunteers from all across the nation and he looks absolutely wiped out during the morning service. He didn't ask for this overload of work. At one point last week, he said he pulled over to the side of the road and rested his head on the steering wheel of his car, tears in his eyes, exhausted. His prayer was simple, "Lord, if you don't help me, I don't think I can do this anymore."

He and the members of his small church are doing an amazing job. Their work drains the church bank account as well as their emotional energy banks. Yet Pete encourages the congregation to remember the words of Jesus, "Whatever you do for the least of these you do for me." And he asks them to do a resource evaluation. What do you have that God can use—a camper, a spare car, a spare U-Haul, a forklift, money, how about your time? His biggest problem on the property is keeping the garbage cans empty. He encourages people to come with such a servant heart that they will just empty garbage cans if needed.

He reminds us that disasters are not planned. Serving isn't just at your convenience. The normal flow of their lives was interrupted so that they can serve. "This is our reasonable service and God has put us here for such a time as this," he adds, quoting from the book of Esther. Strength seems to pour into him even as he speaks. By the end of the service, he looks more refreshed; his own sermon seemed to encourage him.

His church sits on 13 acres and boasts a warehouse behind the sanctuary that was formerly used as a youth building. Today on the church property, several trailers, one housing shower facilities, dot the landscape of the church's park-like setting.

A number of tents house volunteers who have driven in from various states with truckloads of work supplies. Last week, 100 people from 15 different churches slept on the property.

Later, after lunch and a nap at my new abode, I return for the evening worship and communion service, rejuvenated by the badly needed rest and strengthened by the community of a very loving group of people.

Outside the building, I stop to chat with a dozen volunteers from Tennessee and Ohio who are getting ready to go out to eat. They are hearty men with chain saws. Later in the week, volunteers from various California churches are scheduled to arrive. Someone donated a large trailer for their use and it is in the process of being set up on the property. A forklift stands ready outside the warehouse. As soon as a truckload of supplies comes in, volunteers unload it. Others distribute the contents to distribution sites in the New Orleans area.

Some teams go en masse to neighborhoods and offer their assistance to homeowners. A team went to Slidell, Mississippi last week and knocked on one man's door. He turned out to be a National Guardsman who had just returned home to his family after being given a compassionate leave assignment in New Orleans. The military pulled him out of Iraq and onto the home front war zone. He'd had no idea how his house and family were faring in wake of Hurricane Katrina and the tagalong hurricane called Rita. His family is OK; however, the house is a mess—inside and out. He is a mess. Fresh from combat and witnessing Middle Eastern cities and families devastated by war, he faces a similar scene at home. The team of 15 offers to help. He says, "Do you want me to pay you, or how does this work?"

They reply, "No, we're from a church...just volunteering."

The man is deeply moved. He says, "I didn't know that this is what churches were all about."

The team spends more than 12 hours at his house, clearing yard debris and cleaning the damage to walls and floors inside his house. At the end of the day they ask, "Is there something we can pray for you about?" He nods. The team gathers around him, lays their hands on him, and prays for a while, then leaves him visibly strengthened by their love and compassion—something he couldn't get in Iraq. Something he desperately needs now.

MOVING REFUGEES FROM THE SHELTER TO A TRAILER PARK

My FEMA boss calls me and asks me to move from the DRC to the new Baker Street Trailer Park scheduled to open. He wants me to handle the media and try to get some feel-good, positive coverage of FEMA's activities and progress toward resettling the refugees.

Some of the refugees got on buses to other states. One bus pulled up in front of the Civic Center and filled up with families of black refugees from New Orleans. They were now bound for Iowa, where they would be assisted in starting new lives with just the clothes on their backs and a plastic bag full of free toiletries and used clothing. Other buses pulled up, loaded up, and took off for God knows where. Many people refused to go. They were waiting for real homes close by. Many refused to leave the shelter, their cot, their space on the floor of the red-earth south from which their generations hailed.

I drive over in the evening when it is not so hot.

Row after row of white trailers had been pulled into neat lines of at least 50 per row on either side of a main drive that led to the center of operations for the trailer park, eerily illuminated by street lights casting their misty glow upon the vacant village. Not a creature stirred inside the barbed wire enclosed camp. No men with guns here. Just a guard at the gate and barbed wire keeping out intruders who had no business being there. The refugees were being moved from a giant bedroom shared by 500 others sleeping next to each other on cots watched over by National Guardsmen with big guns, to a gated community where each had his or her own shower and a bit of privacy—if not from noise, at least from others staring at them all day every day. It was a little better. But it wasn't a house or an apartment in a thriving city where everyone moved to the rhythm of his or her own life. It was a tin can in a country dust bowl where the lights were always bearing down at night and the relentless sun by day.

They are moving from ashes to dust.

A couple of men stand at the gate, view my badge as I tell them I just want to drive around and see what I'll be dealing with tomorrow. He waves me on in.

YOU HAVE NO IDEA HOW MUCH AUTHORITY YOU CARRY

Tomorrow comes early. I arrive back at the Baker Street Trailer Park to help deal with the media that is due to arrive en masse this morning while residents of the Civic Center board busses and come here. The dust kicks up behind my car as I drive in, thinking this won't look good on camera and imagining dozens of black people walking to their assigned trailers covered in a layer of dust. This won't do at all.

I dodge a couple of logs lying across a street and park near the main tent that holds a huge "Welcome to your New Home" banner draped from pole to pole next door to a pre-fab building that will house something or another. Everything is in flux. Two lead contractors in charge of constructing the site walk over to meet me. One tells me that they have been trying to get someone from FEMA out here for days. They are glad that I have come.

"So what would you like us to do to get ready for the busses?" a man about my age asks.

"Excuse me?" I am confused.

"You're with FEMA. This is a federal installation. You are the highest authority on site," he replied. "We're just waiting on you."

Tag—I, the lowly temp worker, working as a public information officer who has very little power and no actual authority—am it.

"Um, I am just here to deal with the media," I bashfully explain.

"But we've got some serious issues with the trailers that need to be addressed. See, someone at FEMA just gave us a list of people moving in, but they have listed a family of four being in a trailer for two and our lists don't match their lists," he continues on as my cell phone rings.

"Excuse me for a moment," I reply as I step away from him.

It is someone from the FEMA news desk inside the JFO. He tells me that the people don't want to get on the busses at the Civic Center. They are afraid that if they move into a trailer, they will be stuck there and never moved into permanent housing. It will be hours before they can get the mess sorted out and move them to Baker. The media is hanging around the Civic Center, waiting for the outcome.

Well, not all the media. At that moment a couple of cars race up in a dust cloud and park by the welcome tent. A cameraman with CNN prominently displayed steps out. More follow behind him. *Damn. They are here.* I walk over and tell them the story is at the Civic Center and to come back later. They talk amongst themselves, reach for their cell phones, and race off again.

I turn to the site managers and tell them I will call FEMA and get the housing people to come down here and straighten things out. I don't know who to call so I call my supervisor. He promises to pass along the news.

"Look Julia, I'll try to get some people out there by 4:30. Hey, I know you are in the hot seat out there but you are just there to handle the media. Try not to get involved," he says.

I feel the levy of pent-up frustration springing a leak. *Try not to get involved!* I want to scream! But I know that it is just as intense for him inside the JFO away from the sights and sounds and smells of a restless sea of humanity as it is for me, so I steady my voice and say, "Okay. Thank you," and hang up. The site managers are watching me. I may be there just to handle the media, but in my mind that involves setting the stage as well.

"What did he say?" one asks.

"He said they are gathering all that they need and hope to be out here by 4:30 this afternoon. Meanwhile, it looks like I am in charge until they get here."

Someone needs to step up. And, according to them, I am the ultimate authority on site.

"What would you like us to do?" he asks.

"Well, do you have a water truck that can go along these roads and keep the dust down?"

He brightens. "Yup, we got one on site."

"And can you get those logs out of the middle of the road?" He nods. "And what else do you think needs to be done before the people arrive, besides straightening out the housing lists?" He names a few things and I say, "Great. Go for it."

A group of volunteers is already on site to help welcome the refugees and move them through the paperwork and sign-in process; get them a package of dishes, utensils, and cleaning supplies, and help them carry it all into their new tin home. Some of their shirts identify them as being part of a Calvary Chapel. Others, with their Asian-like faces, dressed in long saffron balloon pants and orange shirts say they are from some Yogananda group in an obscure country. They barely speak English and make up for their lack of language skills by smiling broadly whenever I look their way. Some are white couples from the surrounding suburbs here to help, so they say. I think they are here to see what kind of neighbors they are getting. They look a little worried.

We all settle down and wait. The day passes. No one comes.

By mid-morning of the following day, the busses trickle in. FEMA has personnel on site to deal with housing issues. The media falls in place and I give them the FEMA spiel of background information, lend a few golf carts to those who have been establishing relationships with me over the past few days—the BBC and CNN crews who want to chase people down for exclusive interviews inside their new homes.

The Jim Lehrer News Hour has sent a producer, reporter, and cameraman. Reporters from Reuters, The Baton Rouge Advocate,

AP, NY Times, the BBC, and the New Orleans Times Picayune arrive with photographers in tow. Finnish Broadcasting has sent a team of two. News crews from ABC, NBC, WAFB (local), WBRZ (local), WLFT (local), and, of course, CNN.

Later, crews would arrive from AFP, a French news wire service, NBC national, WDSU-6, a New Orleans station that is somehow up and running. CBS shows up with a two-man crew.

A producer from The Morning Show comes over seeking background information. I cannot tell her much. For some reason, I am being kept in the dark and given only information on a need-to-know basis—and that, only when I call in desperately seeking answers to questions I am constantly asked.

MORTUARY SERVICES AND UNCLAIMED BODIES

In the middle of the media frenzy, I receive a call from a CNN producer who wants to know the current body count in New Orleans and the location of the mortuary services field office. She asks if I know how many unclaimed bodies there are. She tells me that many families have opted not to claim the bodies of their loved ones. They cannot afford the burial costs. So they walk away and let the dead bury the dead. I refer her to the news desk. I am not equipped to deal with questions about the dead. I am here to serve the living.

No doubt, mortuary services would photograph and catalog the bodies and cremate them or take them to some mass gravesite. I have no idea and I don't want to know.

PUBLIC PRAYER, WITNESSING, AND FREEDOM OF SPEECH

A couple of the young volunteers from Calvary Chapel walk over to me and one young man boldly says that the construction supervisor who is overseeing the volunteers told them they were not allowed to pray with people or do "house blessings." They were told that I am the Federal representative and had the ultimate say in the matter.

I listen to their agitation and laugh. They look surprised, and it dawns on me that they are probably thinking that I am mocking them or going to boot them off the grounds. So I hasten to say, "This is federal property, paid for by the tax-paying public. And last I heard, the people still have freedom of speech on land that they technically financed. You have total freedom of speech. However," I cautioned, "be discreet. These people have been through a lot. If they want to talk to you about God or pray then fine; if they don't, please respect them and move on quickly. Also, try not to pray too publicly—especially in front of the media. Keep it inside the trailers and you will be fine."

Their eyes light up and they eagerly rush off to tell their comrades while I go smooth things over with their overseer. I tell him what I told them and he seems a little miffed despite my explanation that FEMA partners with many faith-based organizations to provide shelter, food, and other response services. The government knows the fact that volunteers will likely want to share their faith with others and that is part of the package.

Later, one of the construction site managers struts over to me and says he is wondering if I gave the volunteers permission to proselytize on federal property and would like me to explain how I could let them speak so freely when there is supposed to be a separation of church and state.

He doesn't know that I am somewhat of an expert on the subject and that I actually wrote a book some time ago about the Engle v. Vitale Supreme Court case that coined the phrase "Separation of Church and State." So I launch into a gentle lecture saying that neither FEMA nor the Feds are funding the building of a church on this property and compelling the residents to join it, neither are we paying the volunteers to preach, so we are not establishing a state-sponsored religion here. Also, the nature of federal property means that taxpayers own the land.

Last I heard, we still have freedom of speech in this country—on private and public land—and so we cannot tell these volunteers what they can and cannot say. They are not employees—they are volunteers.

It sounds reasonable to him. Then the orange balloon pants of a Yoganandi volunteer passes into his field of sight and he nods at the man and says, "Well, what about those volunteers?"

I reply, "They have the same rights to freedom of speech while they are on American soil." Then I wink at him and add, "But I don't think they speak English."

He laughs, then wanders back to his job. But about an hour later he returns with a worried look on his face. He tells me he had walked by a trailer and heard a few volunteers in there with a black woman praying really loudly.

"Who was praying the loudest?" I ask.

He glances down at his feet sheepishly and says, "The woman who is assigned to live in the trailer."

I laugh and remind him that what goes on in a resident's "home" is none of our business. He nods. The debate is over.

UN-MEDICATED AND UNDOCUMENTED MEDICAL NEEDS

Over the next couple of days, Mayor Nagin swings through with the paparazzi preceding him. Admiral Thad Allen, who has taken over Katrina recovery operations and has his office at the JFO, follows him a day later. The media is all over him, too. At this point, I relinquish all responsibility for managing the media to the Admiral's public relations people. It is good for them to see this trailer park. I am glad that they came.

Later in the week, the trailers seem full. It is my last day here. The media have come and gone. FEMA got their feel-good stories on the national and international news. The water truck continues its daily routine of keeping down the dust. The pre-fab room becomes a medical center. As I walk toward the center, I see a skinny, Caucasian older gentleman, wearing a brown corduroy jacket and carrying a box of something. He looks like a professor, clearly out of his element and nervous about being here.

He is a psychiatrist contracted by SAMSA through FEMA funding, here to see who might need some medication. The box contains psychiatric meds. He is walking around in a trailer park full of un-medicated city people, addicts, and criminals with a box of drugs. I think it best to pull him into the medical center, which no doctors or nurses seem to have yet inhabited, and have a chat. I give him the names of the local governmental appointees who are to handle medical and psychiatric appointments and trying to track down records from demolished hospitals. I think it is not safe for him to be walking around with a box of drugs in this neighborhood. He agrees and drives off in search of his colleagues.

As he drives off, a black woman in her thirties comes into the center with her elderly mother leaning on her arm. They sit in the chairs established in the waiting area of the room. "Is this the medical center?" the daughter quietly asks me.

"Yes, but there is no one here until tomorrow," I reply glancing at the older woman. "Is this an emergency?"

"No. She just needs some help but I think it can wait until tomorrow."

I reach for a sheet of paper hanging on the wall listing local doctors within driving distance of a mile or two and the number for emergency services. "If she needs some medical attention today, you can call any of these numbers," I say handing her the sheet.

She takes it and looks at her mother's slightly vacant eyes staring into space. The older woman seems fearful, yet barely comprehending what is going on. She either has some dementia or she is retreating far inside herself, the trauma affecting her fragile brain chemistry in such a way that psychosis has begun to infiltrate and carry her into a place from which she may never return. Then the daughter looks down at the floor, overwhelmed by the responsibility. She reaches for her mother's hand and sits in silence.

I do the only thing I can do for them at that moment. I pull up a chair on the other side of her mother, take her hand in mine and sit in silence beside them for a long while, praying silently, until my strength flows into them and they feel ready to walk on—taking one more step toward another who might enter into their silent traumas, reach out for their hands and lead them, finally, home.

NEW ORLEANS AND MARTIAL LAW

That night I drive back to my host's home in Baton Rouge and decide to take the next day off. I need to get out of the dust bowl and have a great idea for a diversion—a little road trip into New Orleans. Tina has wanted to go in and see her home city. Some of the other church ladies want to come along, too. Their husbands don't want to go near the place. They are a little afraid but they will let their wives go.

Walking in the door of Tina's house, I say, "Come on girl—it's road trip time! Let's go see ground zero! I've got tomorrow off."

She makes some calls and the next morning, four ladies from the Vineyard Christian Fellowship pile me in a van and wave goodbye to their worried husbands.

We drive down the freeway into a section of town that bore the brunt of flooding. High water marks line the buildings like soap scum. Cars rest at odd angles on lawns, over curbs, sideways, and upside down. Their paint is corroded to a dusty grey that looked like the dust of nuclear fallout or the ash of an erupted volcano. There is so much work to be done on this part of town that it looks impossible. The lower ninth ward and other parishes are still pulling bodies out of the muck. Priorities lie elsewhere. Still, we hear the chain saw of some homeowner whose restlessness will not allow him to wait for helpers to come alongside him.

Driving down St. Charles Street in the Garden District, the ritziest street in New Orleans full of southern historic mansions and ghosts, the rank odor of decay wafts through the open windows of the car. The power had been out for several weeks now. In front of every house sit two or three refrigerators, sealed up like servants bound and gagged, waiting on the sidewalk to be taken away. Brick façades blown down by the wind lie in heaps of rubble beside old churches and mansions. Piles of tree limbs stacked along the road double head high. Someone has been at work. The wealthy could afford to hasten their recovery. The poor would likely never recover.

Suddenly, I spot a photo op and shout at the driver to stop! "Pull over! It's photo time." I shout as their heads whip around to discover what new devastation I seem to have spotted. Several bottles of booze and a bright yellow, brand new laundry basket sit on top of a low retaining wall at the edge of a mansion lawn. "Quick," I say to Tina. "Perch yourself over there on that little retaining wall by the booze and hang your head in your hand like you've just had enough." She laughs, leaps from the car, and plops herself down on the wall beside a half-empty bottle of Findlandia, an unopened bottle of Bloody Mary mix, a sickeningly green bottle of apple something. A plastic laundry basket of plastic dishes lies at her feet with a few more dishes strewn along the wall for effect. Another surreal scene—plastic dishes and bottles half-full of booze are neatly tucked into a brand-new laundry basket sitting on the retainer wall outside a mansion. Who would have thought to leave it there and why, was yet another of New Orleans' mysteries. The staged street photo doubles us all with stress-releasing laughter. My bladder can't handle it. I really needed a bathroom.

LOOTERS WILL BE SHOT

We head for Canal Street where we know there will be at least one hotel open. As we drive along, every business we pass is all locked up, their windows bearing the ominous words splashed hastily in white paint, "Looters Will Be Shot." The phrase seems catchy. Others use it all over the city. In some parts of the city, looters have been shot. Many have died. Stories abound of triggers pulled by National Guardsmen and other sanctioned and unsanctioned security forces "keeping the peace."

Private security people hired by the wealthy drive back and forth along St. Charles Street. Armed men roam the city streets. I don't know why my friends' husbands were worried. Everyone seems armed here to protect against looters—except us. And we definitely do not look like a gang of looters so we're safe.

We turn into Canal Street's wide and vacant lanes, park the car and stroll down the main shopping street, still treacherous with debris, devoid of the masses that once scurried down the sidewalks shopping or businessing, only an occasional car passing rather than the steady stream of traffic.

Muscular men over six feet tall wearing civilian clothes and military style pants patrol with even bigger guns. Something marks them as police but I doubt it. They appear to be a hybrid—all fathered by Arnold Schwarzenegger's character in *The Terminator*—half police, half special ops military personnel from the looks of them, bred especially for this purpose of keeping order among thieves and looters. I don't ask who they are and where they come from. And they don't tell. They are probably more Blackwater men. They don't even ask for my credentials, who I am or why I am here. They look at this small group of white, middle-aged women, see no threat, nod at us, and walk on. We are the only people on that once-thriving shopping street. We can walk down the middle of the road if we want to…so we do. We walk on a ruble-strewn street that is usually bumper to bumper with inner-city traffic.

Walking into the closest hotel that seems slightly dark but open, I try to nonchalantly pass the security guard with Tina. He stops us anyway, asks if we are staying there. I don't answer the question, merely state that I am with FEMA and show him my

FEMA badge. He lets us pass. Apparently, FEMA people are staying at this hotel alongside media and God knows who else. The only thing we care about is using the toilet. At least my FEMA credentials are good for something. They get us into the toilet.

From Canal Street, we get back in the car and drive slowly toward Bourbon Street. We begin talking about the possibility of global climate change being responsible for the hurricane and wonder if they will be stronger and more frequent as the years go by. I pipe up, "Untrue! We all know it was President Bush who caused this hurricane." We all laugh.

It is true that the United States is becoming more vulnerable to natural hazards mostly because of changes in population and national wealth density as more people and infrastructure have become concentrated in disaster-prone areas. It is also true that natural disasters are growing more frequent and severe—especially floods and cyclones. However, earthquakes remain steady. To what degree is climate change involved in this? I don't know.

I do know that it will take every American to be willing to respond to disasters in the years to come. If one part of the country is affected, the unaffected ones will need to go to the part that is impacted. It is time for us to not only reach out to one another in our own community but to be willing to take a step farther. None of us can do it alone or go it alone.

We must hearken back to the days when everyone turns out for a good old-fashioned barn raising and release the help of all for one and one for all. County people are great at this still and have the heavy equipment to assist during natural disasters along with practical sandbagging and chain saw wielding skills. City people worry me by their lack of a sense of community, their ideals of self-preservation, and focus on developing skills that are rendered meaningless during a disaster. The government is encumbered by protocols that create difficulty responding to more than one major disaster at a time. It has never even faced the magnitude of a disaster like Hurricane Katrina. During the time state and federal governments worked together to coordinate a response, everyone was on their own for the first week. The first to respond to the actual victims of the disaster were locals and volunteers—from outside the city. The first shelters to open were private homes and churches—mostly in the country. The next wave brought in volunteers from across the nation.

It used to take a village to help one another. In this millennium, it will take a global village.

THE FIRST TO START SINGING

We pull into a parking space just off Bourbon Street and park. The French Quarter looks fine—high and dry and all cleaned up. A voodoo shop has reopened that day. Another souvenir shop down the street is open with its walls lined with multi-colored plastic beads for revelers who are certain to return en masse. And a bar. But it doesn't feel like the movies portray—no bead-swinging crowd of merry revelers dancing in the streets. Few people walk through town. And then there is us. The sober church ladies growing more silent as they walk the streets and turn into Jackson Square Park. A lone palm reader has set up a table at one corner of the park as if he isn't allowed inside the park where he and dozens of other occultists, craftspeople, and musicians usually liven up the scene.

New Orleans after the storm lies still and waiting.

"I've never seen it so empty and quiet," one says as they all sit down on benches. No one speaks for a while, each lost in her own thoughts and memories.

I consider all that I have seen and heard over the past few weeks and realize that I've been working in the midst of some of the most traumatized people on the planet, drawing on all of my counseling skills to handle the media and individuals throughout the day.

Here in Louisiana, 500,000 displaced people are longing for a home that no longer exists. They are now disaster refugees, climate refugees, on the road to a new life they never wanted. Trauma is trauma. We'd better get used to seeing it increase in the world and on American soil. We will all be called to respond one day, locally or far away. We are the stewards of our time and place. If we don't care for one another, our souls will erode until we lose our sense of compassion that keeps us human.

Eventually, Tina speaks up and shatters our reveries with her genteel New Orleans accent. "Ah nevah knew there were birds in this park. They must have been drowned out by all the human noise and musicians that are usually here. Ah've nevah heard them sing here before."

Apparently, after a storm, the birds are the first to start singing. And we were the second to launch our songs of worship and prayer to the heavens above Bourbon Street, after the storm.

I wrote this just after leaving New Orleans. Now, many years later, I feel like we all need to understand that major disasters impact peoples' lives long after the media leaves. We will always have tornados, hurricanes, earthquakes, and floods. Whole communities may be demolished in a matter of minutes. You may live in one of the communities.

If you live in a disaster-prone area, are you and your family prepared?

Are you prepared—not just to survive for a week until electricity and food become available again, but for a month? Are you prepared to be relocated? The time to prepare is long before you are caught up in the storm.

If you do not live in a disaster-prone area, are you prepared to use your skills and gifts to reach out and help others? You may be just the right person needed at the right time. Your church may be called upon to take up the challenge of becoming a shelter, or a center for recovery operations. Are you ready for that degree of laying down your lives for 30 days or more?

The centuries have always had their share of droughts and famines, climate disasters and earthquakes. How did the first century church respond to those disasters? How should we?
Read on...

CHAPTER 3

PRACTICAL PREPARATION FOR THE DAYS AHEAD

by Julia Loren

Throughout history, God spoke to His prophets about times to come, often through visions of doom and gloom. He gave Daniel visions that actually traumatized him. These visions were so graphic in detail about the future of the world that afterward, an overwhelmed Daniel took to his bed and cried out in intercession asking for an increase in understanding the days that God revealed. Other prophets cried out and asked God to stay His hand after they heard or saw what was to occur in the days to come. The apostle John also saw troubling visions about the end of days, days that some people believe are upon us now.

Although you may not see the biblical prophets who speak of doom and gloom as "prophets of hope," they can be. It depends on how you interpret their words. God's words release hope *if* you hear the word of wisdom hidden behind each word and understand how you are personally called to respond. When people gather together and hear a word that sounds like doom and gloom, everyone responds differently. Some only hear the gloom. Others see the glory about to unfold.

Word got around one particular city that a meeting would be held at a certain believer's house—a meeting you wouldn't want to miss that would certainly encourage the ever-growing ranks of Greeks in Antioch who had become followers of Jesus. They were becoming known as "Christians," the latest fad to hit the religious scene, a fad that turned its backs on centuries of Greek god and goddess worship for a single man who was said to have raised himself from the dead and releases spiritual gifts. They called their gifted oracles "prophets." Several of them had arrived from Jerusalem and the meeting in Antioch would be amazing.

Who knows how many gathered that night? Some sat on the floor with their eyes wide open taking in the scene, while others sat with their heads bowed, listening, praying, their spiritual senses heightened by the presence in the room, the air pulsing with the energy of the Holy Spirit combined with their anticipation. Surely God was about to speak. One of the men, known for hearing accurately about times to come, a man named Agabus, broke the tension as he stood and began to speak. Through the Spirit, he predicted that a severe famine would spread through the entire Roman world (see Acts 11:25-30).

The presence of God (the Holy Spirit) filled the room and touched each listener's heart as if whispering, "Listen, this prophet is speaking a word that could only come by revelation from Me. What he is saying is true." And so they listened and talked among themselves about what a famine would mean to them and to their brothers and sisters in the region that would be most impacted.

Their response turned a gloomy prophetic word about an impending disaster away from being a word of judgment and transformed it into a word of hope and redemption.

WHAT DOES THIS MEAN FOR YOU?

Imagine with me, for a moment, what those men listening to Agabus immediately thought. I imagine that one man thought, "What does this famine have to do with me? Famines happen all the time. My family will be unaffected, so why should I be concerned? God helps those who help themselves."

Yet another likely thought, "It is the judgment of God upon them. Everyone knows their ruler Claudius is corrupt in thought and deed and hates the Jews. Who can avert God's judgment and why should we? They need to repent. The rain falls on the just and the unjust alike."

Another perhaps thought, "The tenderness of Jesus caused Him to reach out to feed the poor and heal the sick, so this is certainly not His will that people should perish. If they were my family, I'd want to make sure they were well protected. This is a wake-up call for me to become prepared for the outbreak of famine, war, emergencies, and disasters that could occur in my area and reach out to others during times of need."

One individual likely immediately strategized about what to do. "Jesus was certainly a practical prophet. He took loaves and fishes from a little boy and multiplied the food source. We could take what little we have and send it to them. We should send our fellow believers, our brothers and sisters in Christ, some money to build up their food supply while the community is still selling commodities. We have very little time. If the famine happens next year, they need to buy during this harvest season."

A businessman in the room probably thought, "How can I use this information to invest wisely so that I can help secure the future of my family for the coming generations, my community, and wherever else God calls me to give to the body of Christ in the future? Jesus spoke about the 'talents,' investing wisely to multiply the resources that He gives us. Surely, He will grant me wisdom to create wealth and, like Joseph, have the foresight to store up those resources and dispense them in the future."

As they talked among themselves, the word of wisdom came through consensus and they decided that a collection must be taken and sent to the region through a trusted envoy. Who better than Barnabas and Saul to deliver both the money and impress upon them the reason for the gift?

That night, several things became clear: God is not the God who wills disaster, but a God who provides before the disaster even happens because God knows when it is about to occur. God knows how to meet the needs of His people before they even know they are needy! And God continues to speak through His prophets. The prophetic word of doom became an avenue of hope and redemption for many whose lives and livelihoods were saved because true listeners are not just titillated by words from God, they take it to prayer and community and seek God for how they should respond. Those who knew the true nature of God—that God is love—responded in love and action.

It takes a listening community who is tuned in to His voice and has taken stock of the resources, natural and spiritual gifts that each individual among them carries. And it takes a word of wisdom to know what to do with the things that you hear.

FINDING YOUR STRATEGY AND PURPOSE

But what if those listening to the prophet's word simply stood up and appealed to the God of Love and used their authority to stop the famine through prayer? We respond according to the level of our faith and how we perceive the Lord. The same Holy Spirit resides in us as it did in Jesus. When Jesus stood up in the boat and rebuked the wind and the waves, who was He rebuking? The enemy and his plans for destruction. Are we not filled with the same power and authority? Or do we believe that things are already set in motion and are fixed to a cosmic timeline so we cannot calm the storms, divert the winds, or stop the raging seas and erupting volcanoes? Who are we colluding with—the plans of the evil one who is hell-bent on destruction, or the plans of the Lord for total redemption and healing of the peoples and the lands of our global home?

Let's go back to those fictitious men who I imagine listened to the prophet's word about the famine. The first man failed to listen, failed to prepare, and his heart was more focused on himself than filled with compassion and wisdom. God only knows what happened to him. The second thought God's will was to judge and let them all perish. The third prepared an emergency food supply and disaster plan for his family in case they might have to flee from some future disaster. His heart felt peaceful because he knew that he was prepared. Another man developed a response and recovery plan that enabled whole communities to mobilize and reach out in the love and compassion of God to others who would be impacted. Hundreds and thousands of people came to know the love of Jesus and enter into the salvation of Christ because of his outreach. The last man, the businessman, knowing that food prices would rise as energy costs soared, invested in the stock market, made a fortune off misfortune, and reinvested the earnings into companies that would mitigate against future losses for entire communities and minimize damage. He acted not just to enrich himself or to assist only fellow believers. He used his investment for all humankind, including those who had no faith in any God, because he was filled with the love and wisdom of God who cares for all of Creation. He also knew that crisis meant opportunity and he shifted his emotions and thoughts into productive avenues and action. But perhaps one man, Paul or Barnabas or an unknown new believer, could have stood up and said, "No" to the famine and averted disaster.

Now, come with me out of the book of Acts and into New Orleans, Louisiana in August 2005. I was there, in the aftermath. Just like the men in Antioch who heard the word of an impending natural disaster, people responded differently to the prophetic words God released to many prophets before the hurricane ever hit.

Many Christians heard or read the words of well-known Christian prophets who predicted a storm would hit New Orleans. A couple of prophets "saw" New Orleans underwater, predicting the levies would fail. One Baton Rouge pastor told me that prophet Bob Jones said that his church would become the epicenter of recovery after New Orleans was flooded—long before Hurricane Katrina. His word helped prepare that pastor and his congregation to willingly turn their buildings into a response and recovery center hosting thousands of volunteers from around the nation.

Some Christians said the hurricane was God's judgment. Others said it was the natural consequence of ordinary cycles of hurricanes complicated by poor building planning and bad planning regarding levy safety. Still others, who had heard the warnings, watched in horror and knew that they were being prompted by the Love of God to suspend judgment and act in compassion—for their God is a God of Love and compassion. Businessmen mobilized and rushed around frantically trying to discover the right state and federal contacts who could tell them how they might obtain contracts from the government for the response and recovery efforts. Those businesses that had prepared beforehand already had the FEMA contacts and contracts ready to sign and were prepared to prosper. Pastors stepped up and turned their buildings into shelters and feeding stations. Some opened their buildings to volunteers from around the world who descended on the area with chain saws and practical tools to assist with the recovery. The racial divide was closed for a season as blacks helped whites and whites helped blacks in the initial aftermath.

Hurricane Katrina woke us all up and called us all to respond in some way and our responses revealed what was in our own hearts—judgment, apathy, greed, or love—and how much we reflected the nature of Jesus.

All around the world and even in your own backyard, disasters are likely to occur. What is your strategy to prepare and respond to what may happen to you, your family, and your neighbors? Do you have a plan of action, or even of evacuation?

PRACTICAL PREPARATIONS FOR THE DAYS AHEAD

We are constantly being warned of difficult days ahead. How many Christians are prepared to accept that heartbreaking losses and changes will continue to unfold in their lives and around the world? Christians in every country are being called to shake off their slumber and apathy and discover new strategies for living and transforming the world. Intercessory prayers must be mobilized into intercessory actions.

As for the people of New Orleans, most of them never heard the words of the prophets predicting what was going to happen months before Hurricane Katrina hit. Most did not have the means or preparation to leave New Orleans and so they suffered or lost their lives. A few prepared. One woman I met had gathered a stash of cash and prepared an evacuation plan because she wanted to ensure not just her own safety, but the safety of her children and grandchildren. She gathered them all and fled ahead of the storm as far north as she could. Some failed to listen to the warnings about the strength of the storm. Others never heard the prophetic words that went beyond the newscasts—words that spoke of New Orleans being under water. It should have been a clue that the only way that could happen was for levies to fail. Had the prophets been given a louder voice in the city, had their words been more respected, more lives could have been spared and the response and recovery time greatly improved.

As for the people of New York and New Jersey during Hurricane Sandy in 2012, what did they learn from the climate refugees of Katrina's aftermath? Apparently nothing. Many did not leave. And those who did thought they would return to their homes in a day or two...just like those in New Orleans and Mississippi. They failed to realize that they needed to first of all prepare to be self-sufficient if they were going to remain at home. And second, to make an evacuation plan that faced up to the fact that they may not have a home to return home to. And in failing to plan, the foundations of their lives were swept away by winds and waves.

What do we do with what prophets speak? I believe we should do what they did in Antioch...listen as a community and seek God for how we should respond, not just as individuals, but also as a community of believers—*even for the sake of unbelievers.*

We all hear imperfectly. We all have the same Holy Spirit speaking and yet each one of us interprets what we hear differently. That is why we need to dwell in a community of listeners who can bring their different ways of thinking and different interpretations to the table and listen for the true interpretation of the word of the Lord, and more importantly, what God is calling them to do with that word.

Within 40 years, the coming generation will see a world-wide population explosion that will tax all of our resources. Every natural, technological, or man-made disaster will impact a huge population. It will become more important than ever before to develop community, where people trust one another, where every individual has developed the ability to draw close to the Lord and listen intently and accurately for the word that He speaks. We will need to listen not just for ourselves, but also for one another as never before.

In a sense, we must all become prophets—those who listen, those who receive revelation directly from the throne of heaven and have the history of relationships and accuracy in revelation so well developed that others trust them. They have earned that trust because they have the integrity to not lead others astray with their visions, their dream interpretations, or their revelations. We must become prophets to the unbelievers who seek revelation in non-Christian sources—the psychics, astrologers, and shamans—and release the truth of God's presence, power, and wisdom as we step out in love and compassion.

If we are living in the last days heralding Christ's return, as many believe, it is imperative that you do your own listening. It is imperative that you listen for others—for your family and friends. The call to prayer resounds all over the world in huge prayer gatherings and small community clusters. However, the secret place of your own home is where the Lord speaks more intimately. And those who have developed their own relational history of hearing the voice of the Lord and heeding the prompting of the Holy Spirit will be so tuned in that they may just be the ones who avoid disaster. They may be the ones who get out just in time, with all their family and possessions intact.

YOU ARE GIFTED FOR SUCH A TIME AS THIS

You have a unique way of seeing and perceiving the world. You also have a specific mix of natural and spiritual gifts that you carry within you. Ask God to show you those gifts within you and the gift that you are to the world in this hour of history. You are purposed to be here for such a time as this. God knows the times and seasons in which you live. God created you and longs for a relationship with you and desires to give you revelation of your purpose and future. Take time to interact with the Holy Spirit in these days ahead, and ask God questions. He hears your spoken and unspoken thoughts. Ask for divine appointments and strategy to reach your destiny as you do your own listening. Draw closer to God. Let's move deeper and higher into His presence rather than run away and hide in fear and self-absorption. Let's all become messengers of hope to a crazy world.

God's ways are not our ways. He is not the author of confusion (1 Cor. 14:33). He is one whose perfect love casts out fear—He doesn't cause it (1 John 4:18). His plan is to give us a future and a hope—no matter what happens in the earth (Prov. 23:18; Jer. 29:11). He sends His word to encourage us, to comfort us, and to prepare us for the days ahead. He doesn't send His word to judge us—for Christ came not to condemn the world but to save it (John 3:17). He sends His word to turn our hearts toward Him— not to scare the hell out of us and cause us to think He is evil in His intent toward us. Any words or thoughts in your head about anything other than the supreme goodness of God are twisted lies. True followers of Christ know the personality and nature of Christ. They know that God does not will that any should perish but that all should be redeemed. Jesus is in the seek-and-save business, not the condemn-and-annihilate business.

Do you really know much about the goodness of God and can you access His presence during these stressful days we live in?

I want to leave you with one final thought: The abundant life is about living in the presence of God. During these days ahead, hold on to who God really is: God is Love and God is Good. Inhale His love and exhale His peace. Center yourself there.

PRACTICAL PREPARATION

1. Do you have an emergency supply of cash, food, water, fuel, etc. that will cover you and your family for at least two months in the event of a major disaster in your neighborhood? Do you have a backup plan for escape and sheltering elsewhere should your home be destroyed? Does everyone in your family know who to call if you all get separated, perhaps for days? A point of contact outside of the state can be useful for everyone to call and check in.

2. Does your neighborhood have an emergency planning committee and are you on it? The presence of God in you is badly needed to bring peace and wisdom during times of crisis. Your community needs you to be involved. And it is a great outreach opportunity.

3. What gifts and talents do you have that may be needed in emergency planning or in post-disaster recovery?

Opportunities abound to volunteer and to profit for a purpose. Are you connecting with those opportunities *before* you are needed so that you are all set and ready to respond nationally and internationally?

Part 2

PROPHETIC PROMISES AROUND THE WORLD

CHAPTER 4

THE START OF THE FOURTH WAVE

By James W. Goll

One of the most consistent ways the Lord speaks to me is through the avenue of dreams. Many of my writing and speaking assignments are given to me in such a manner. Prayer assignments over the years have almost always come in the forms of visitations and visions. This is especially true if it is a strategic assignment.

While ministering in Brazil in July 2012, I was seeking the Lord for His mind and thoughts concerning future movements of the Holy Spirit. I went to sleep in my hotel room in Belo Horizonte and woke up out of a "stunner of a dream." The manifested presence of God was riveting on my body as an after effect of this dream encounter. It shook me.

I have yet to tell the full dream experience publicly, but I have been directed to present portions of it to you now. Perhaps I will be released at a later date and the proper setting to actually proclaim the message. For now, I am going to steer away from my craft of interpreting and just bring you the raw message.

I SAW SOUTHERN CALIFORNIA AS A WOMB FOR THE BODY OF CHRIST!

Like an eagle in flight, I was hovering over the globe in search for a place to land. Suddenly the entire West Coast of the United States came before me. I zoomed in upon the state of California and with the eye of an eagle I saw glimpses of redemptive purposes and plans. I then turned in flight over portions of southern California and I saw something that seemed unusual. Southern California was a womb for the body of Christ. She had been used to conceive the Word and the Spirit over the last one hundred years of the church age to bring forth different movements of God.

My "knower" was on high alert as I flew over Los Angeles and Orange County, California—that this womb had already received another word implanted at least a year earlier and that another long-term, almost overdue, birth was imminent. I then soared over Pasadena, California and the next thing I knew the eagle suddenly flew into the historic Mott Auditorium on the hallowed grounds of the William Carey University.

I SAW JOHN WIMBER STANDING ON THE PLATFORM!

Suddenly on the wings of an eagle, I was taken into Mott Auditorium in Pasadena, California. The place was packed with worshiping believers with standing room only. The atmosphere was electric with the presence of God. Rabid worship was happening with occasional authoritative declarations by various leaders. I noticed a few desperate pastors I knew crying out with anguish for God to visit them once again. Then things suddenly shifted.

All of a sudden the late John Wimber, former leader of the Vineyard Movement and voice for the Third Wave, was firmly standing on the newly purple-carpeted platform. The cultural atmosphere was now pregnant with a realm of the glory and the thick majesty of God. Then I heard and felt the voice of John Wimber echo an invitation that rattled the entire place. He simply declared, *"Come again Holy Spirit!"*

People starting crashing to the floor en masse under the impact of the power and authority that resonated on those simple words. Once again another sound wave was released, *"Come again Holy Spirit."* It was not gentle Jesus showing up or the comforting dove of God manifesting. It was not just another renewal or revival meeting, though it seemed include all of those qualities. It was the violent invasion of heaven entering a time and space world. It was a "church quake."

I felt the reverberation coming off the sound waves of the voice of the invitation. It shook the very building, the grounds, and all those present. The fear of the Lord fell and an earthquake of a 5.7 magnitude resulted. The quake resulted in an anointing resting on Psalm 57. "Be gracious to me, O God, be gracious to me, for my soul takes refuge in You; and in the shadow of Your wings I will take refuge until destruction passes by. I will cry to God Most High, to God who accomplishes all things for me. He will send from heaven and save me" (Ps. 57:1-3 NASB).

People screamed in terror as the entire grounds and buildings were rattled by the sound of God's voice being heard and felt once again. Signs and wonders broke out, but it appeared as an after effect, not the primary goal. Then a third time I heard the pronouncement from John Wimber, *"Come again Holy Spirit!"* People crashed to the floor in droves.

As I pen this, I just now realized some things I had forgotten. They just flashed suddenly within me as I compose this. I also saw the late Jill Austin, one of the fieriest prophetesses of the last decade, gazing in upon the happening and smiling. I heard her laugh echo over the occurrence as if to say, "I told you He was coming!" I saw a great cloud of witnesses, including Aimee Semple McPherson and others, gathering around to peer in upon this strange outbreak. The convergence of old anointings still seemingly resident upon California was now colliding.

SUDDENLY I WAS AWAKENED!

My senses were heightened. It was July and I was ministering in Brazil—a land pregnant with revival—but suddenly it appeared to be another season and it was fall, right at the time of the Jewish New Year of Rosh Hashanah. Then pages of a book flipped quickly from one chapter of time to another and suddenly it was 40 days and nights later. I smelled smoke in Mott Auditorium as the place had been filled with the burning fiery sacrifices of violent praise and worship. I smelled burnt flesh. I smelled aromas of life and death simultaneously at work.

Short messages from different anointed vessels were a part of this new sound wave, but again it was not the main thing. Miracles happened. They suddenly occurred. But again, this was not the aim. It was not why the people even assembled. Yes, there were even short passionate pleas and desperate cries for help! But even that was not the central focus. This move of God centered on the radical worship of the One, Christ Jesus the Lord, and the abandoned welcoming of the third person of the Godhead—the Holy Spirit! The jealousy of God permeated the experience.

It was not a conference. It was not even polished. It was not even 24/7 as we presently know it. It was raw and overpowering. It was not rehearsed. It was an invasion of the Holy Spirit Himself.

A window of opportunity had opened and this uncontrollable surging sound wave jumped spontaneously around the globe. A man appeared on a pogo stick gleefully jumping from city to city and nation to nation. The man on the stick was William Seymour of the historic Azusa Street Revival. He leapt across the nations and everywhere his pogo stick landed, light came for a brief moment! The nations were in an uproar and fire and light was falling around the globe.

THEN I HEARD ONE LAST WORD

"A line has been drawn in the sand." Terror gripped me. I shook. I honestly did not know what was coming next. I still do not know, having pondered deeply on this experience. Was it days of Glory or impending societal chaos? Was it times of economic collapse or reformation where a new order was created out of tumultuous uncertainty? I honestly was left not knowing what the outcome or the result was or would be.

But this I knew. Hope for the fragmented Body of Christ and the nations was being released. An invitation was being sent from heaven to earth and a line was being drawn in the sand.

The word went in me. The word penetrated me. The word has disturbed me. But this I know, heaven has a word that must be heard in the earth realm, *"Come again Holy Spirit!"* And the invitation must have an urgent and appropriate response.

WAVES OF THE HOLY SPIRIT

For a few years, I have been meditating on the principles of "Catching and surviving every wave of the Holy Spirit" while yet staying grounded in the main and the plain of the doctrines of the historical church. There have been numerous movements of the Holy Spirit throughout our wonderful church history—the Great Reformation, the First and the Second Great Awakenings, the Pietism and Holiness Movement, the Student Volunteer Movement, the Pentecostal Outpouring, the Latter Rain and Healing and Deliverance Movements, and even in more recent times, the Evangelical and Charismatic movements, and many others.

Every wave of the Holy Spirit has restored truths to the larger Body of Christ and often even birthed entire new denominations and or ministries. The first mention of the Holy Spirit is that He moved "upon the face of the deep" (Gen. 1:2 KJV). So going by the Law of First Mention in biblical interpretation, we can say it is the nature of the Holy Spirit to move and keep on moving.

I have seen or experienced the following expressions of the Christian faith in my own span of 60 years: Evangelical, Charismatic, Jesus People, Discipleship, Word of Faith, Third Wave, Global Worship and Prayer emphasis, then shifting into the Prophetic Movement and the New Apostolic Reformation. Within each of these tidal waves there have been the contributing revival peaks such as the Korean Church Growth, Argentine Outpouring, the Chinese Underground Church Movement, the Cell Church explosion with its many expressions, the Toronto Blessing, Brownsville Revival, and many other contributing tributaries.

THREE RECOGNIZED WAVES IN THE TWENTIETH CENTURY

The Third Wave is a term that was coined in the early 1980s to describe the recent historical working of the Holy Spirit in the global Body of Christ. It is part of a larger movement called the Neo-charismatic Movement. The Third Wave involved those Christians who had received Pentecostal-like experiences. However, those who identified with this movement often claimed no association with either the Pentecostal or the previous Charismatic movements.

The "First Wave" occurred at the beginning of the 20th century with the rise of the Pentecostal movement, arising in Topeka, Kansas in 1901 with Charles Parham and shifting to the Azusa Street Revival in 1906 with William Seymour, Frank Bartleman, and others. This gave birth to many classical Pentecostal denominations such as the Assemblies of God, Church of God, Foursquare, Church of God in Christ, Pentecostal Holiness, Open Bible, and various other Pentecostal streams. Other revival movements came on the shores in various parts of the earth as in Wales under young Evan Roberts; Shantung, China with Bertha Smith; and the Hebrides Islands with Duncan Campbell and many other lands.

The "Second Wave" occurred during the 1960s as the Charismatic Movement spread throughout mainline protestant denominations as well as the Roman Catholic Church. The Full Gospel Businessmen's Fellowship, Women's Aglow International, the Discipleship Movement, and Word of Faith Movement were also expressions of this massive global wave. A parallel movement, based on the West Coast of the United States, was the birthing ground of the Jesus People Movement with the signs and wonders of Lonnie Frisbee and teacher Chuck Smith of Calvary Chapel. Contemporary music had its debut with Maranatha Music leading the way with a host of other expressions following in its amazing trail.

The "Third Wave" occurred during the mid 1980s and into the 1990s and was associated with leaders such as John Wimber of the Vineyard Movement, along with others such as James Robison, C. Peter Wagner of the Church Growth Institute and Fuller Seminary. They were a part of the Baptist Fullness Movement along with many other significant voices of integrity with sound theology such as Jack Deere and others.

MOVEMENTS IN LIFE TIME

In 1960 in Van Nuys, California, the modern Charismatic Movement began in an Episcopalian Church (St. Mark's, with Dennis Bennett as rector). There was an outburst of tongues-speaking in this church. This event was so significant that both Time and Newsweek covered the story. After that, the movement spread like wildfire in the Episcopalian and Anglican Church—and then among Lutherans, Presbyterians, Methodists, and other mainline denominations as well.

At the time of spring vacation in 1967, there were in the Notre Dame area about 30 zealous Catholics who had received the "baptism of the Holy Spirit." In 1970, the increase was more spectacular. Almost 1,300 attended the conference, including Catholics from Canada. In 1973, 22,000 Catholic Charismatics met together at Notre Dame, including Catholic participants from at least 10 foreign countries. By 1974, the Notre Dame conference was attended by 30,000 people. It simply grew and grew.

The Charismatic Conference on Renewal in the Christian Churches was held in Kansas City in the summer of 1977. I was a young leader in the Jesus People Movement in attendance at this grand event. I will never forget the spontaneous praise that broke out for over 20 minutes as Bob Mumford declared, "I looked at the back of the Book, and guess what? We win!" It was an electrifying moment!

All three wings of the Pentecostal movement were present: 1) Classical Pentecostals; 2) Protestant Charismatics; and 3) Catholic Charismatics. This was the biggest and most inclusive gathering of "baptized in the Spirit believers" in modern history. There were nearly 50,000 participants in this five-day historic conference.

THE SIGNS AND WONDERS MOVEMENT

The Fuller Seminarian C. Peter Wagner first coined the term "Third Wave" in 1983:

> I see historically that we're now in the third wave. The first wave of the moving of the Holy Spirit began at the beginning of the century with the Pentecostal movement. The second wave was the charismatic movement, which began in the fifties in the major denominations. Both of those waves continue today. I see the third wave of the eighties as an opening of the straight-line evangelicals and other Christians to the supernatural work of the Holy Spirit that the Pentecostals and Charismatics have experienced, but without becoming either Charismatic or Pentecostal. I think we are in a new wave of something that now has lasted almost through our whole century.[1]

I also had the honor of crossing over into this Third Wave emphasis after being a participant in both the charismatic and Jesus People ripples, as I had the honor of being a part of the leadership of Metro Christian (later Vineyard) Fellowship led by Mike Bickle in the heartland of the US. It was a time of the mingling of the anointing of compassion and worship of the Vineyard with the prophetic and intercession of the Kansas City prophets. Multiple streams of the Prophetic Movement emerged quickly in many locations and continue to flourish to this day. This in turn was succeeded by another step of restoration that some refer to as the New Apostolic Reformation with many diverse global networks and expressions.

THE BEGINNING OF THE FOURTH WAVE

In the spring of 2011, I was given a vivid prophetic dream in which John Wimber was the central figure. This great Third Wave leader had already graduated to his heavenly reward in 1997. This musical minister was one of the greatest statesmen who moved in authentic power in recent church history. In this stunning dream, the Holy Spirit used John Wimber as a representational voice of the Third Wave. I was told that the purpose for that movement had now subsided and that it was time for another wave to roll in upon the scene of global church history.

A conversation with the Holy Spirit unfolded and it was explained to me that the previous waves included renewal, revival, and empowering of the Holy Spirit and aspects of restoration. It was shared with me though that there was a "fresh movement" now emerging on the world scene that would include all of the previous ingredients of the earlier movements as it was a time of the Convergence of the Ages. I heard, "It is time for the Fourth Wave to crash upon the course of history." This Fourth Wave would be one marked by transformation.

Please take note that the previous three waves came from or had great influence in California. So would it also be with this new Fourth Wave. It is, and will have, great impact in California but be global in nature. Some of our older leaders in the Body of Christ would now be free to graduate to their heavenly reward while others with youthful and teachable hearts would be invited to be the fathers and grandfathers and mothers and grandmothers as "Reformational Architects."

The Fourth Wave emphasizes societal change by channeling these empowered believers to impact the seven cultural mountains of religion, government, education, business, family, media, and the arts and entertainment. Fresh intercessory strategies will now arise for effective ministry in the marketplace and beyond. The supernatural power of the Holy Spirit gifts will not be able to be contained within the four walls of the church, but rather will explode into every sphere of life. Apostolic hubs in numerous cities of the earth will emerge, each with distinct assignments of influence releasing rippling supernatural effects into the different spheres of culture.

Let it be known, that from a view from my chair, the Fourth Great Wave has begun!

Dr. James W. Goll is the president of Encounters Network, the director of Prayer Storm, and the director of God Encounters Training. James is the prolific author of numerous books including *The Seer, The Lost Art of Intercession, The Coming Israel Awakening, Deliverance from Darkness,* and many others. www.encountersnetwork.com

Note

1. C. Peter Wagner, "The Third Wave?" Pastoral Renewal, July-August 1983, 1-5.

CHAPTER 5

A DECADE OF REALIGNMENT

by Martin Scott

There is no question that the world is changing and changing fast. The clock helps us understand *chronos* time, but this decade does not seem to want to keep in step with the clock. It's a decade of rapid change, a time for kingdom advances. At the beginning of the decade I had a dream, the latter part of which was simple yet profound. I watched a 20 and a 10 come down from the sky; the numbers fell onto a seesaw, with the 20 on one side and the 10 on the other. Instantly the 20 outweighed the 10 and the seesaw was unbalanced. Then came an 11 that replaced the 10. It dropped on the seesaw and there was a major swing, but back it went as the 20 still outweighed the 11. This pattern continued for each digit—12, 13, etc.—right up to a situation where a 20 came and there was a 20 sitting on both sides. Then as it settled, the seesaw was balanced.

We are in a decade of great swings, with a constant attempt to pull things back to the status quo, but by the end of the decade there will be major re-alignments. Our world will look different. Why the realignment? I consider this is due to the Living God who answers prayer. Why the swings back to the status quo? Probably due to two factors: a human (and a church) desire for the familiar and also the work of the enemy to confuse, intimidate, and cause fear to rise. It is paramount that we guard our hearts against fear; "Let not your hearts be troubled" is a word for this time. We must also resist the temptation to run to the familiar for cover. Uncharted territory lies ahead, yet in that uncharted terrain is the invitation to enter into the level of first-century God-experience expressed in a twenty-first-century context. Our participation with God will allow us to live through some of the most wonderful shifts that can be recorded in history.

For some time I have had a quote from Rudolf Bahro on my screen that I have often read:

> When the forms of an old culture are dying, the new culture is created by a few people who are not afraid to be insecure.

Culture is always changing, but there are certain times in history when there is a major shift in culture. This is such a time. At a national level we have to see this cultural change take place. Legislation is vital, but the real battle is a cultural one. Laws will be broken, but culture is what shapes a people. Culture acts like an unwritten boundary. Compassionate and just culture that is shaped through godliness is what our lands cry out for. It is also vital that we become committed to impact culture globally. I am very skeptical about most of what is written of "the antichrist" and such things, but am very aware that into vacuums will come something or someone to fill the space. The ultimate outcome of the triumph of the kingdom is certain; the immediate generational outworking is in the balance. Change always occurs, but does not always occur at the same rate, and again we are alive at a time when the pace of change and therefore the opportunity to affect that change is in our hands.

The days of church as a ghetto are ending. The days of embracing and loving our communities—from within and as part of those communities, releasing change—are here. For the world to change the church has to change, and the church cannot change without two wonderful dynamics coming together. The presence of heaven and the love for the world. The former has been increasing; now the fear barrier has to be broken so that the latter can increase.

THE SHAKING OF ALL THINGS

Knowing the ways of God will help us interpret what we experience. God answers prayer, but the answer to prayer is not a straight line. When we pray for our faith to rise, the most likely result is that we face trials. In other words there is a *process* toward the answer that is released when we pray. Hence a new order being established in the Spirit will come through what has been established being shaken (see Heb. 12:28) or (in the language of the dream) through the swings of a seesaw.

There are always fresh outpourings of the Spirit, but we have lived through a century when the Body of Christ has experienced the effects of three global waves of Pentecost. We have also lived through signs such as the Berlin wall coming down, and the tragedy of the twin towers, as well as traumatic tsunamis and earthquakes and weather patterns that seem out of control. All this speaks loudly; surely creation is crying out. The cry is always one for liberation from bondage and into the purposes of God.

Shifts seem to have two "sides" to them. The positive and what can seem like the negative. We receive a kingdom that cannot be shaken (positive) through everything being shaken (the process that can appear negative). Realignment means everything will be shaken.

What we have been praying into will help us understand what is taking place. There has been a cry for the power of God, and we are very grateful for the increase in the miraculous. There is more to be experienced, but the calling out to heaven has begun to have a bigger effect than we anticipated. There is healing for bodies and there is also healing for nations, which comes through the cross.

THE SHAKING OF IMPERIAL POWER

Let me begin with a big one. The shaking of imperial power so that true power can be manifested.

> *In the fifteenth year of the reign of Tiberius Caesar... during the high-priesthood of Annas and Caiaphas, the word of God came to John son of Zechariah in the wilderness* (Luke 3:1-2).

Luke the historian is interested in more than dates and personalities. He is interested in recording the impact the presence of the kingdom of God is going to make into the world that was dominated by the Caesars of Rome. He, like his fellow followers of Jesus, knew that Caesar, despite the claims from Rome, was not "lord." A process began in the desert with John; it comes to decisive fulfillment in Jesus as He breaks religious, economic, and political power in Jerusalem in order to pour out the Spirit on His people for testimony in the world. As we read Luke's follow-up book, we realize that he leaves the narrative unfinished. He leaves us with Paul under house arrest in Rome, proclaiming the kingdom of God. The world where Caesar claimed he was lord was the very same world where Paul made his declarations that Jesus was Lord. There is no mistaking the deep parallel of Jesus ending in Jerusalem and Paul ending in Rome. Both teach from the Law and the Prophets concerning the kingdom of God. Jesus deals with religious power, thus unlocking a proclamation of transformation for the world.

Essentially, nothing has changed since that time. Caesars are no more, yet there are many claimants, personal and corporate, to the title of "lord." We are still on the same trajectory, making proclamation that all peoples belong to Him. I have in my spirit that there is much to be done and brought to a climax back in Jerusalem. Not simply because it is a holy place, but because this Gospel has always been destined to run through the whole earth, purifying people and land alike. I believe we are in a major time of acceleration of that process. In the western world, that acceleration means we will see the people of God poured out into the world in ways we have not seen before. Certain church institutions will become more marginal to God's people as the Body finds heavenly permission to carry the presence of God with them. Meanwhile, a major shift is to take place in the Muslim world with women at the forefront. And (but not in an exclusive sense) Jerusalem in some way acts as a homing beacon. God is not finished with the Middle East, but the whole world is His, not some square miles in one specific place. So the drawback to Jerusalem will be marked by decentralization where the church has been established and the raising of the marginalized. This will not be to everyone's liking or expectation, but is the precursor for waves of His presence to come.

The challenge and critique the prophets gave to Israel was, "Who is your Protector?" and "Who will be your Provider?" Whenever the nation was judged, it was normally over those two core issues. Jesus likewise presented the same challenge to His disciples. He sent them out as "lambs among wolves." I can almost hear them say, "But do you know what wolves love to eat?" So if God did not protect them they would become fodder. Likewise, He challenged them over provision: "Do not take a purse or bag or sandals" (Luke 10:4). Travel light, and trust God.

In the Western world historically the church has often been favored, having a privileged position. By 2020 much of that will have gone. Why? We are going to find again that He is the Protector and the Provider. There still is more work to be done within the Body to prepare for finances to transfer so we will continue see financial squeeze on ministries. Jesus, always the radical but always the benchmark, in choosing Judas to look after the money was sending a signal for all who follow that people are a higher priority than money.

Finances are coming, but the seesaw will swing. Fresh emphasis will come on the use of finances. Great entrepreneurs will rise who carry the spirit of humility but have a vision for national transformation. In 1991, I had a vision: from the nations, those believers who handled finance met together and through prayer, wisdom, and the prophetic God began to give them strategies for working alongside governments for economic restoration. At a time of economic shaking, this is the opportune time. The increase of those with economic expertise who will be working to develop social enterprise in less-privileged lands will abound.

Love for a nation is vital and love for a neighborhood must be present for change to take place in that neighborhood, but the love that God is releasing is a global love that has a local outworking. This process is going to bring about a fresh kingdom alignment and challenge where we simply have national alignments.

There is a work taking place—redeeming a people for the King from all the nations. Great harvests are coming in the places we have not anticipated it. Among the Muslim people a harvest is gathering momentum. Harvest too is coming in the Western world, but the shift He is calling for is an alignment so that we see His harvest field as the world. Days of church restoration of course will continue, but the agenda has shifted. The future shape of the church will be determined by the world. Like water poured out, it will find the lowest point, and the pouring out of the people of God is now on us. He has poured into us, He has called us into the river, but now there has been a shift. The greatest days ahead are not the days of conferences and within the four walls, but the days in the home, the street, the office—the days beyond the four walls.

A running back to the familiar will cause a slowing down of our entrance to the future and leave us with only some nostalgic memories of what used to be. We need to feel insecure; we must feel that if we are to help create a new culture. Not the culture of church, but the culture of the Body of Christ continuing to do and to teach what He began (see Acts 1:1).

A good working definition of imperial power is that *it is marked by an empowered few who promise benefits to all who comply with the system, but the true benefits flow back to the few.* This can take place in a very visible fashion, in say a dictatorial setting, and can also take place in the benign setting of church life. Jesus said of this kind of power, "But you are not to be like that..." (Luke 22:26). Increasingly, this will be judged in all its forms. The future is not the localization of the gifts in a few but the distribution to the many.

The faceless, nameless ones will arise; or rather God's activity through them will only increase. "Aslan," we read, is not tame.[1] Neither can His followers be tame. The shaking of imperial power means that even structures that have served thus far will begin to crumble. The transition to the fresh manifestations will not come neatly and simply through old structures changing. Many new and even strange things will begin to emerge outside of apostolic boundaries. That is the nature of the wildfire of God. Apostles did not shape the work of God in Acts; they were normally a step or two behind what God was doing. He was the boundary-breaker, and this again will be a hallmark of the next years.

THE MUSLIM WORLD AND WOMEN

Early in 2009, the Lord spoke to my wife and me to pray for and to watch the women of the Muslim world. He said that they will be a sign that breakthrough is coming, and they will be the means of breakthrough coming. We have been amazed, in what has been termed the "Arab spring," at the vocal presence of women.

A new love for the Muslim world is coming and must come. In the west there has been a righteous rising up against the evils done to the unborn, but recently the Lord spoke to my spirit a word that shocked me. He said that when we dehumanize people the end product is the dehumanizing of the life in the womb. The prayer and campaigning about abortion will also have fruit to bear in the love that will come for those of different ethnic backgrounds. Fear will be overcome by love.

AN ECONOMIC WORLD IN CRISIS

Leadership will come forth. Africa is coming into a new season of producing leaders for the coming years. Political and Christian leaders will arise from there, but also Africa will produce leaders who make a serious level of contribution into the banking world. New systems are going to be developed that will not be reliant on current structures and we will see the basis for currency exchange change.

All of this could be very threatening, but it is the environment for the socially-conscious entrepreneurs to rise. Innovation will seem like a gift from heaven that has been unlocked. Problems, even ecological ones such as waste disposal, will be answered with creative responses.

Economically there is a major shift coming. Tighter in the pocket, but more adventurous in spirit will be the result to the people of God. Having less but releasing more. There will come a wave of teaching about stewardship, and with it revelation as to the stewardship not just of the money in one's own account, but the wealth also that is within God's world.

CONFUSION OVER WHO IS FROM GOD

A great phenomenon is going to take place where there will be a number of those like Cyrus who will be "secular" leaders but anointed by God. Although not believers, they will be raised up to carry His purposes forward. They will even at times speak as though they are prophetic voices. This will cause confusion to those who have been taught to look at everything through a Christian lens, rather than seeking to discover the purposes of God.

At the same time, though, deceitful public figures will arise. The discernment of those will be necessary. They will often say the same thing as the Cyruses, but carry a different spirit. The hallmark that will distinguish the true from the false will be humility. God has been cleansing church leadership of pride, and there is a wave that is coming into the political arena likewise that will humble the prideful. As we see judgments of this take place, it will train us in our discernment to know when it is a Cyrus who is speaking.

Likewise, there will be those who rise with a spirit of betrayal. Jealousy will mark them. In all of this we are going to learn that we do not look to the "top" in terms of human position, but that we have to look higher to the One who appoints. We are not to be thrown even when we hear of mainline teachers who are living in compromise. It is the era of the unknown stepping forward who know the Living God and fear Him above all else.

Another sign of God at work on the margins will be a number of prisons that will be visited by God, who will come to inmates and staff alike.

WHAT A TIME TO BE ALIVE

A decade of shifts, re-balancing, and realignments. A decade for those who walk through the barriers erected by the fear of consequences. The land that God invites us into will always produce good fruit, and that good fruit as always will be guarded by giants. Who we listen to will make all the difference. Opportunities can be taken or missed for a generation. Fear and a desire for the familiar will rob us, but an adventurous excitement about God's activity will pull us to new heights. The decade will release wholesale changes. We can hold on to what we have and find a diminishing return or sow it into the future.

Martin Scott carries a passion and great hope for the continent of Europe, believing that a radical shift within the Body of Christ will bring a freedom to express the Gospel beyond the four walls. Since 2009, he has lived with his wife Gayle in Spain where they are seeking to close ancient doors of bondage as they connect with Paul's apostolic prayers for that land, and also find new ways to express the historic testimony of Jesus. He believes the best days are the ones ahead, challenging ones, but ones that will enable or force us to discover the truths of an apostolic Gospel. http://3generations.eu/blog

Note

1. Aslan the Lion is considered to be a fictional portrayal of Christ Jesus. "'Safe?' said Mr. Beaver; 'don't you hear what Mrs. Beaver tells you? Who said anything about safe? 'Course he isn't safe. But he's good. He's the King, I tell you." C.S. Lewis, *The Lion, the Witch, and the Wardrobe* (New York, NY: Harper Trophy, 2000), 80.

CHAPTER 6

A FIELD OF DREAMS OR NIGHTMARES?

by Rick Joyner

While praying about the future of our economy, I was given a vision of a long, lush green field. I felt that this represented a long period of economic prosperity, which has generally been the case since that time. While praying in August of 1995, I saw this field in a vision again, but with much more detail. The end of the field was covered in fog. Not far into the fog there was a very steep cliff. In the middle of the cliff, there was a narrow, twisting, steep path that appeared like a descending bridge. It had the same green grass on it that the field did and went all the way to the bottom.

Those who walked into the fog almost all missed the little path and fell over the cliff. Some of these died, but nets below the cliffs caught many of them. However, these nets were not there to save the people but to trap them. Others entered the fog carefully, dropping to their knees and searching for the path, which they seemed to intuitively know was there. Most of those looking for the path were able to find it and carefully started down on their knees. A few people had parachutes, and they jumped off the cliff into the fog.

At the bottom there was a sea with four kinds of ships in the harbor—slave ships, warships, luxury liners, and hospital ships. Most of the ships were slavers. The next greatest number was warships. There were only five hospital ships, all of which were on clean, well-kept docks right in the middle of the harbor. The two luxury liners were docked at each end of the harbor. An abundance of supplies were on their docks, but both the docks and ships looked filthy and poorly maintained. No warships were docked, but all kept moving about in the harbor.

The people who fell into the nets were put on the slave ships. Most of those who made it down the steep paths headed for the hospital ships, but many did head for the luxury liners. Of those who headed for the luxury liners, some were captured and made to board a slave ship.

The luxury liners were closely guarded, and obviously under the control of the warships. The warships occasionally took people from the slave ships and luxury liners, and they were taking whoever they wanted—they could not be resisted.

Those from the hospital ships were also taking people from the other ships. However, they only took the weakest or those who were so sick or wounded that they were not expected to live.

The crewmen of the hospital ships were shown respect because they wore brilliant armor that seemed to confound everyone else. Those who were jumping off the cliff with the parachutes were all landing on the hospital ships or their docks.

When a slave ship would fill up, it would depart, making frequent turns as if it knew where it was going. The warships were also making so many turns that it seemed impossible to tell which way they would go next. Any ship that happened to be in the way of a warship when it turned was blasted and sunk by the warship. If the warships turned toward each other, they started shooting at each other until one was sunk.

Because of the fog, many ships collided with other ships and sank. The water was filled with sharks that quickly devoured those who fell into it. The confusion, despair, and fear over the harbor were as thick as the fog. When the fog thickened, these fears would intensify. When the fog would thin a little, hope would begin to rise in the people. When the fog lifted enough so that the open sea could be seen, the ships would begin heading for it.

The hospital ships were also the only ones who seemed to be sailing as if they knew where they were going. They could sail right through the chaos in the harbor and into the open sea at will. One or two of them were constantly going out to sea, disappearing for a time, and then they would return. Then another would go and do the same.

As I followed one of these ships to the open sea in the vision, all of a sudden it was as if I was standing on the bridge of the ship. The farther out we went, the more the sky cleared. Soon it became bluer than I had ever seen it, except when flying in a high-altitude jet. I was so intrigued by the sky that I had not been watching the sea. When I looked back at it, I saw that we were actually flying at a very high altitude.

I thought that we were going out into space, but soon we descended toward what appeared to be a whole new world. It was composed of islands, each with a different culture of people on it. The wounded on our hospital ship were placed on several of the different islands, so that each wounded person was placed with those from his or her own culture.

These islands were at perfect peace, and there were beautiful white bridges connecting them to one another, with a constant flow of people on the bridges. On each island vast foundations were being laid for a great city.

Even though each island was very different, and different from any place that I had ever seen, I felt immediately at home on each one. They were each like paradise, and though they seemed to be on a different world, I knew that they were somehow very close to the one I had just left.

INTERPRETATION AND INSIGHTS

That I can now see the end of this field indicates that the end of our economic prosperity is now in sight. What I saw at the end was much more catastrophic than I had ever thought. There are some very dark times ahead, but at the same time there is a whole new world being built right in our midst that is more wonderful than we can even imagine.

To the degree that we have built our lives and faith on the economy of the world, we have built on a very shaky foundation. We know that the time will come when everything that can be shaken will be. The time that we have been given until that happens is for the purpose of preparation. Let us build our hope and trust on the kingdom that alone cannot be shaken.

Those who kept walking into the fog just as they had been walking in the open field, not discerning or not acknowledging the change, either perished or fell into slavery. Those who immediately fell to their knees found a safe way down, but it still led down. They had to stay on their knees all the way; no one could have stood up on that slope because it was too steep and narrow. Falling to our knees speaks of prayer. As soon as we see the fog, or confusion, we must pray for every step we take thereafter.

That no one ascended, but all went down to the bottom of the cliff, spoke to me that the economy of the whole world was going down. Many will survive what is coming, but not at the level they are presently. Much of our present standard of living has been built upon credit, borrowing from the future, and the future is now here. We are fast approaching the time when the bills will have to be paid. That will cause a drastic reduction of our present lifestyles.

I felt that the slave ships were banks. During the Great Depression, banks were so overextended that most of them failed.

Somehow, they have now positioned themselves to not only survive another economic collapse, but will actually be in a place to enslave those who are in debt to them.

The warships were all different sizes, and I felt represented different powers. Their efforts were not coordinated, but they all seemed to be in as much confusion as everyone else, and all seemed to be at war with one another. They lived by plundering the other ships and each other. I believe that in the times ahead, small wars will be flashing up almost everywhere and without apparent reason. Anyone who gets in the way of those with some power will be in trouble.

The luxury ships were so filthy that it seemed only slightly better to be on one of them instead of a slave or warship. It was obvious that the luxury of the future will not be as we know it today. Also, the luxury ships were constantly being plundered by the warships, making them almost an intolerable place to be. Even a hint of luxury in the future may only serve to make us targets.

I knew that the hospital ships were the church. They were glistening white with red crosses on them. They were so bright and clean that they stood out dramatically in this vision. White speaks of purity, and the red crosses spoke to me that they were bearing the cross. Red is also the color of sacrifice. These ships were so beautiful that anyone would have wanted to be on them. The church will become the most desirable place in the world to be, and the church will become the pure vessel she is called to be when she takes up the cross, committing herself to the life of sacrifice. In the times ahead, the life of sacrifice and service to others will be the most desirable life in the world and will actually be a glorious place to dwell.

The people on the hospital ships each wore brilliant, silver armor. They, too, stood out dramatically whenever they appeared, and this caused everyone to show them great respect, even the warships. This spoke to me that when believers learn to wear their armor, they will command the whole world's respect and have authority because of it.

The docks of the hospital ships were also spotless and were overflowing with supplies. There was far more wealth on them than on the luxury ships, but the wealth was being used for service, not luxury. Because the individuals with the armor and the hospital ships commanded such respect, no one was trying to plunder their great stocks of supplies, even though they were obvious to everyone.

When a hospital ship pulled between two warships that were fighting, they would stop fighting and give them their wounded. It seemed that this was one of the primary purposes of these ships, to simply stop the fighting whenever they could.

In the midst of the chaos of this place, the dignity, resolve, and purpose that the Christians and their ships moved with was stunning. The greatest feeling came over me when I stood on the bridge of the ship leaving for the open sea. That feeling was freedom. As soon as we entered the open sea, we ascended into the heavenly places. Once out of the fog, we did not travel on the earth. When we came back down, it was to a seemingly new earth, even though I knew somehow that it was right in the middle of what I had left.

That I entered this extraordinary freedom on a hospital ship speaks of finding our true peace when we take up our crosses to serve others. When we do this, we will begin to dwell in the heavenly places. Then we will see the earth very differently—we will see what God is doing. I really felt that those paradise islands were already right in our midst, but we just could not see them yet.

At the very time when the world descends into a terrible chaos, which will probably begin with economic chaos, God is building bridges between people that will be the foundation of a glorious future. The end of this age is the beginning of the one over which Christ will reign. In Revelation 17:15 we are told that, "The waters which you saw where the harlot sits, are peoples and multitudes and nations and tongues" (NASB). The sea often represents mass humanity in prophetic language. That the sea at the bottom of the cliff was in the most terrible chaos represents what the kingdoms of this world are headed for. The islands represent that the Lord is also laying a foundation for His kingdom right in our midst at this same time. That I knew these islands were close to the sea of confusion spoke to me that what the Lord is about to build on the earth is also very close at hand.

The bridges are right now being built between people. The bridges were for interchange, and it was obvious to me that each island was building something wonderful, as if it were the very best from their culture, in order to share it with the other islands. That new foundations were being laid for cities represented a whole new beginning for the earth. What is now being built for the Lord, for the sake of His kingdom, will remain and be a foundation for the age to come.

Rick Joyner is the founder and executive director of MorningStar Ministries and Heritage International Ministries and is the senior pastor of MorningStar Fellowship Church. He is the author of more than forty books, including *The Final Quest, A Prophetic History*, and *Church History.* He is also the president of The Oak Initiative, an interdenominational movement that is mobilizing thousands of Christians to be engaged in the great issues of our times, being the salt and light that they are called to be.

Rick Joyner, "A Field of Dreams or Nightmares?" (MorningStar Prophetic Bulletin 75) December 10, 2012. Used by Permission. www.MorningStarMinistries.org

CHAPTER 7

THE COMING OUTPOURING IN EUROPE

by Julia Loren

During a long and revelatory worship set on November 20, 2011, the Holy Spirit took me up and into a vision where I "flew" over Europe and saw the territory the Lord had marked out for the outpouring of His Spirit in the coming years. (For an explanation of these types of visions, please see *Shifting Shadows of Supernatural Experiences* by James Goll and Julia Loren, published by Destiny Image.)

On the first pass through Central Europe, the Lord took me back to places where I had been in recent years—particularly in Germany and Italy. He then rolled back the memories and said that ministry will look very different in the years to come in Europe. A sovereign move of God will flow like a spring snow melt that begins with a trickle as the initial snow pack melts, then gains strength and rushes and roars into various watersheds for a season that will change the face of European Christianity.

The Lord showed me that as Germany is the first nation to fully embrace the move of God in Central Europe, the rivers of Germany will carry the rushing waters into other countries. I saw Germany come alive in the Spirit and the Lord said, "As Germany goes, so goes Italy." And as the fire of God's love consumed them, they spread the word through Austria and the spring thaw rushed over the Alps into Northern Italy. I also saw the Swiss-Italian border watershed capturing the flow of the Spirit. Then I heard the Lord say, "Look to the university towns of Germany and Northern Italy for a revival among the youth who will carry it throughout Eastern Europe." I believe this includes Heidelberg University in Germany and Padua in Italy (the second oldest university in Europe, where Galileo taught).

As I flew along the Danube into Budapest I saw the crystalline image of a silvery angel hovering above Budapest. Showers of silver rained down upon the Danube and flowed to the east. And wherever the river flowed, revival flowed. For the Lord is redeeming His people out of the ravages of oppression and into the total freedom of the Holy Spirit. The silver and the gold are His to give where He pleases and it is time for the Eastern European bride to step forward, out of the ashes and into the adorning grace of redemption. He has set His gaze upon you. This is the time of your favor—Slovakia, Hungary, Croatia, Serbia, Bulgaria, Moldova, Ukraine, Romania—you who live where the Danube flows.

Then the Lord took me over the United Kingdom where the cross was superimposed across the landscape. I saw four fires being lit—one in the north, one in the south, one in the east, and one in the west of England. And the Lord said, "I am lighting a ring of fire around England and Wales. And I will be a ring of fire around them. Look to four churches to become well-known apostolic resource centers in the coming years. They will release the torches that all of England will either be drawn to or repelled by." And the fire of God will protect them.

Then the Lord said, "Look to the locks that are opening canals long closed." The re-opening of canal locks in the UK is a sign that the ancient waterways are opening that have held back a move of the Spirit of God. New pathways of the Spirit are opening; new opportunities to spread the Word within the region are opening. As the locks become unlocked, the restored waterways of revival and evangelism will emerge and flow.

I looked this up online after receiving the vision, and read a note of significance concerning the ancient locks:

> A whole weekend of celebrations marked the completion of the Droitwich Canals on Friday 1 July 2011, 72 years after they were officially abandoned. ...240 years after they first opened on 27 June 1771, the newly restored waterway is the final link in a brand new "cruising circuit"—the Mid Worcestershire Ring. The Ring allows boats, cyclists and ramblers to make a 21-mile circular journey through some of the UK's most beautiful and historic countryside, from the Worcester and Birmingham Canal to the River Severn, through the city of Worcester and back to Droitwich.[1]

In the 1770s, when many locks were being built or restored, England was in the middle of the John Wesley revival. It is also interesting to note that in 1939, when many canals and locks began closing, history records that World War II broke out that year. Also, religious historians believe that in 1939, one particular man brought Wicca out of the woods of England and spread its popularity throughout Britain and America, launching a Wiccan revival. It seems like 1939 was a good year to close off the waterways of the natural and spiritual enemy. But now is the time to reopen the waterways of the Spirit and let revival break out!

A ring of fire around the country and a ring of locks within it speak of the coming invasion of heaven becoming more manifest than ever before to ordinary believers and unbelievers. Both speak of complete circles—like a wheel within a wheel—and both are signs that the Lord is moving to restore the rich heritage of the Spirit in the UK.

The vision ended and two questions rumbled through my mind. The first was this: Will Europe experience its Spring thaw this year? And the second question was this: As the Lord sovereignly and suddenly lights the fires of revival and evangelism, who will rise up and carry the torch to the neighboring nations? I believe it will be those who say, "Here am I, send me!" who will go to the surrounding nations, and many who are displaced or students living outside of their home countries in Central and Eastern Europe will find themselves riding the rivers and carrying the torch wherever the river flows.

I believe that this is something we all need to be praying—that God will awaken hearts to know His love and compassion, His healing power and presence throughout the UK and Europe. My prayer is that God would release the fullness of His presence to students, and that He would send others to reach out to university students in the UK and Europe. We don't know God's timeline for revival; however, we can prepare by asking God for strategy and individual leaders to emerge quickly—strategy that He initiates so that we can co-labor with Him to prepare for greater presence and power and outreach.

Note

1. Gemma Bolton, "Droitwich Canals Finally Open for 'Business'" IWA: The Inland Waterways Association, July 5, 2011, accessed August 07, 2013, https://www.waterways.org .uk/news_campaigns/campaign_news/droitwich_canals _finally_open_for__business__.

CHAPTER 8

PREPARING THE ATMOSPHERE IN THE NATIONS

by Sharon Stone

Throughout the Scriptures we see God giving instructions to the people of Israel on how to win their battles through prophetic revelation (see Josh. 6:2-5; 2 Chron. 20:15-17; 2 Sam. 5:23-25). Today, we are also facing a battle; not only for our own personal destinies, but also for the destiny of Europe and for our nations. Once again, we need God's revelation concerning atmospheres, territories, strategies, and timings.

Beginning in 2012, Dr. Sharon Stone presented a ten-year plan for the transformation of the spiritual atmosphere above Europe at a meeting of her network, Christian International Europe. This plan was based on what God had been showing her prophetically about shifting the atmosphere above nations for sustained revival and awakening.

Although Dr. Stone received this revelation specifically for Christian International Europe, I believe that it is also significant for the greater Body of Christ in Europe. The areas that Dr. Stone deals with are not comprehensive. Each one of us will undoubtedly be able to think of other issues that are important—national reconciliation, abortion, economic crisis, families, etc.

Our goal in publishing this is to:

1. Create awareness.

2. Humbly challenge leaders and all members of the Body of Christ in Europe to pray and to seek God about which of these areas He would have them adopt as churches, organizations, and individuals, both in prayer and to act upon.

Transformation in Europe will not be quick. It is, however, possible. We will be able to make a difference as we pray and act.

On behalf of the Netherlands Prophetic Council,

ARLEEN WESTERHOF
Netherlands Prophetic Council

BREAKING THE POWER OF RESTRICTIVE AND DELAYING ATMOSPHERES

This is a message which involves atmospheres, territories, strategies, and timings. When Moses sent out the spies to spy out the land, ten of them came back with a negative report: "But the people living there are powerful, and their towns are large and fortified. We even saw giants there, the descendants of Anak!" (Num. 13:28 NLT). This report created an atmosphere of fear and doubt in millions and postponed the fulfillment of the promise of God for a nation for 40 years. Here in Europe we are dealing with restrictive and delaying atmospheres. For many believers it seems as though the fulfillment of God's promises for their own lives and for their nations is continually being postponed, and they are becoming weary while waiting.

There are several strategic focuses that God has given me for Europe which are allowing these restrictive and dangerous atmospheres to continue. (This is not an exhaustive list, and of course there are other major areas of concern: poverty, abortion, family values, economic crisis, etc.) The areas are:

1. National alignment with Israel

2. Modern-day slavery

3. An underdeveloped young generation

1. NATIONAL ALIGNMENT WITH ISRAEL

How a nation treats the Jews and Israel will determine how much authority and blessing that nation receives from God: "I will bless those who bless you, and whoever curses you I will curse; and all peoples on earth will be blessed through you" (Gen. 12:3). God Himself has set the boundaries of the land of Israel as a covenant to the people of Israel: "I will establish your borders from the Red Sea to the Mediterranean Sea, and from the desert to the Euphrates River..." (Exod. 23:31). God does not break His covenant. In the same way, we cannot separate Israel from their covenant land.

> *On that day, when all the nations of the earth are gathered against her, I will make Jerusalem an immovable rock for all the nations. All who try to move it will injure themselves* (Zechariah 12:3).

It will not be easy for our nations to align with Israel, and sometimes it will feel like a heavy stone that we have to carry. This will be increasingly true as public opinion turns against Israel. God, however, is getting ready to move in Israel. God is going to judge the nations and glorify His people, just like He did when the Jews were in Goshen and Egypt.

2. MODERN-DAY SLAVERY

The Bible says that righteousness and justice are the foundations of God's throne (see Ps. 89:14), and it is time for European social reformers like William Wilberforce to rise up again and abolish human trafficking (modern-day slavery). Human trafficking is the illegal trade of human beings for commercial sexual exploitation or forced labor. Conservative estimates show that there are currently approximately 27 million people being trafficked.

Slavery is a moral issue and compromises the atmosphere of freedom and righteousness that God so desires. We need to realize that modern-day slavery does not just exist outside of our borders. As believers we carry a powerful message of hope and liberation.

God commands us to seek justice for the oppressed. Our fervent prayers can accomplish much. We must also understand that God has given us authority and influence through Christ Jesus. We as believers therefore have a special position when it comes to the work of abolition. Through prayer and acts of service we can help rescue and restore those who are being trafficked and help to create new futures for the vulnerable.

3. AN UNDERDEVELOPED YOUNG GENERATION

Developing a Passionate Generation to Guard the Gates of Justice and Sustain Awakening and Revival

Several European nations have experienced awakenings and revivals before. Unfortunately, they were relatively short-lived and not sustainable. One of the reasons for this is that they were not generational. As leaders, we have done a disservice to our youth by leading them to think that we could preach them into revival. We have got to be passionate about the presence of Jesus. We need to expose our youth to dynamic passion and teach them how to guard it and to grow it. We do not just get this from a 60-minute service on a Sunday.

When Moses and Joshua went up to the mountain to meet with God, they did not know how long they would be there (see Exod. 24:12-18). God did not say anything for the first six days. They were, however, content just to sit in His presence. Then, on the seventh day, God invited Moses into the cloud. Joshua, on the other hand, had to remain on the outside for another 33 days. During these 33 days, Joshua got hungrier by the minute for the presence of God.

> *All the people saw the pillar of cloud standing at the tabernacle door, and all the people rose and worshiped, each man in his tent door. So the Lord spoke to Moses face to face, as a man speaks to his friend. And He would return to the camp, but his servant Joshua the son of Nun, a young man, did not depart from the tabernacle* (Exodus 33:10-11 NKJV).

Young people are passionate and proactive. They get angry and frustrated, and they are disappointed when they look at the world. As a consequence, they are often among God's most blunt and unintentional prophets. Jesus asks us to have prophetic foresight, to dream of what a better world would look like, and to work toward the transformation of this world.

It is essential that we equip this emerging generation to be radical, passionate leaders who:

- know the weight of the call of God on their lives and who walk in it,
- who refuse the status quo of religion,
- who seek to explore the depths of God, and
- who live devoted to a lifestyle of worship.

If we do, they will become a passionate generation who will guard the gates of justice in our nations and be able to sustain the coming awakening and revival.

Sharon Stone has been used by God to mobilize the prophetic and apostolic throughout Europe and internationally. Through preaching, revelation, training, and coordination of various national prophetic roundtables, Sharon has strengthened the Body of Christ to advance the Kingdom of God. She serves as the president and founder of Christian International Europe (CI Europe). Her ministry facilitates the CI Europe network and helps empower people through the understanding of their purpose and calling. She carries an authority which shifts and transforms regions. www .cieurope.org

CHAPTER 9

THE ROAD FROM ASIA
TO JERUSALEM

David Demian with Stephanie Muzyka

It was more than ten years ago that the Lord first began speaking to me about the role of the Chinese in His end-time global purposes.

I was invited by Pastor Ernest Chan, a well-known American Chinese leader, to speak at a large conference he was hosting in Los Angeles in July 2001. Many Chinese believers would be attending from all over the world. I was seeking the Lord about what to share in the meeting when He asked me a question.

"What hinders My kingdom from being established in the Middle East, David?"

Having been born and raised in Egypt, a Muslim nation, I knew very well.

"It's the fear of persecution and the fear of death," I answered.

"Yes, but I have a prepared a people," He continued, "a remnant of My Body who have no fear of persecution or death. It is the Chinese people, and they will have a very special role to play in seeing the end-time destiny of the Jews and the Arabs being released."

I was stunned by this revelation. My heart has always been for my people, the Arabs, and through my journey in Canada, God had also given me a heart for the Jewish people. But I had never seen any connection between this and the Chinese.

When I shared what the Lord had revealed to me in the meeting that night, the presence of God came in an unusual way. It was as if we were all captured in a divine moment of sovereign revelation. In fact, Ernest was so stirred that he immediately encouraged the people to sow into printing one million CDs of this message, to be shared throughout the Chinese world. On the spot, all the money was raised.

But when we went to the professional company who was producing the CDs of the conference, the recording of my sharing was completely blank! All you could hear was my voice praying at the beginning, then silence throughout my message until I came to the closing prayer. As soon as I said "Amen," the recording began again.

We assumed it was an equipment malfunction, so my friend and pastor Gideon Chiu, who had been videotaping the meeting on his camcorder, suggested we could take the audio from his tape. But when we looked at the tape it was the exactly the same story—just as I began my message, the tape went blank and the recording never resumed until just after I finished.

My first thought was that this was warfare from the enemy. But then the Lord spoke to me clearly saying, "It is not the time for this message to go wider yet, David."

So I left this conference knowing there was something profound about the destiny of the Chinese, but I wasn't sure what, where, or when the next step would be. A few months later, Pastor Ernest invited me to join him for some meetings he was having in Asia that November. I prayed and I felt the Lord said to go. Before this, though, I was scheduled to speak in an international conference in Israel.

Then September 11th happened. The airline schedules were in chaos and all the new airport security measures were causing huge delays. It was not an easy time to be an Egyptian flying to Israel. So I asked the Lord if I should cancel my trip. But He answered that I must go because there was someone I was supposed to meet there.

At the conference I had many meetings with many people, but at no time did I get the clear sense "this is the person" I was supposed to meet. So I came home mystified.

A few days later, Pastor Ernest called, saying he had received a message from a Taiwanese pastor who had just met me in Jerusalem and wanted me to speak in his church during the November trip.

Suddenly I remembered this man—he was supposed to leave to go back home before I arrived, but the post-9/11 airline problems had delayed his return by a couple of days. So he "happened" to be there while I was speaking. After my sharing he asked to meet with me, but because he didn't speak English we had to communicate through a translator. When he told me he was from Taiwan, I mentioned I would be traveling there in November and he had asked if I would speak at a leaders' meeting at his church. I didn't think much of it—he seemed like a very nice man and I thought maybe he was the pastor of a small church who would like me to encourage his leadership.

"David, do you know who this man is?" Pastor Ernest continued. "Pastor Nathaniel Chow is the founder and apostolic overseer of a movement with more than one hundred daughter churches worldwide. He is one of the most respected and trusted leaders in Taiwan." At that moment I realized the Lord was up to more than I could understand.

I will never forget this meeting in Taipei, which was a gathering of the movement's leaders from all around the world. As I began to share about the destiny of the Chinese, suddenly my translator (who I later found out was Tony Tseng, the president of Good TV, the only 24/7 Chinese Christian TV station in the world) started weeping to the point he could no longer continue. The rest of those present were also so overcome that they came out of their chairs weeping and travailing and lay across the altar and the platform calling out for the destiny of the Chinese.

As I watched this scene unfold, the Lord spoke to me that the day would come when He would gather the Chinese people to worship and seek His face, waiting on Him for His steps to see the destiny of the Chinese fulfilled. And when they did, this would benefit not only the Chinese, but God's end-time purposes for the Middle East and for the Body of Christ globally.

THE JOURNEY BEGINS

I believe that we are now living in the days when the destiny of the Chinese is coming into collision with the timings of God. In 2009 the Lord opened the door for the first Chinese gathering in Vancouver, Canada during Rosh Hashanah. One thousand believers gathered to worship and wait on the Lord without a man-made agenda or schedule. The Chinese are masters at planning and scheduling, but for this gathering they chose to lay aside these natural talents to allow His Spirit to completely direct the meetings. And the Lord honored their obedience by His manifested presence. And He used this gathering as a seed to birth the first global gathering of the Chinese in Hong Kong in May 2010.

In the first Hong Kong gathering, the Lord focused on uniting the five thousand Chinese, attending from Asia and around the world, into one Body as a prophetic sign of His desire for the greater Chinese Church. As the remnant who attended obeyed and waited on the Lord together, He released a spirit of repentance that broke through traditional barriers between streams and nations and caused the hearts of all those present to be knit together as one true family. At the end of the gathering, all those present stood and declared prophetically, on behalf of the wider Chinese Body of Christ, "The Chinese are one family! The Chinese have come home! Back home to the Father!"

The next year, the Lord released another call for believers from Asia and around the world to gather in Hong Kong during the Feast of Pentecost, June 8-11, 2011. And He gave this promise from Jeremiah 32:39: "I will give them one heart and one way" (NKJV). Twelve thousand believers from more than thirty nations responded to this call. During the gathering, the Lord challenged the Chinese to lay aside their own agendas and plans and surrender their lives unconditionally to Him. His desire was that this act of corporate surrender would become a seed through which He might restore the miracle of one accord (divine unity) into the Body of Christ worldwide, preparing the Bride for her end-time mandate and hastening the Lord's return. As all those present stood and covenanted by faith, I believe a beachhead was established in the spirit realm for the sake of the Body of Christ worldwide.

In 2012, fifteen thousand believers from many nations once again met in Hong Kong for the "Kingdom Come" gathering, August 1-4, 2012. Before God's Kingdom can be established in the world, first He must secure His rule and reign over a remnant of His Body. And the Lord used the Chinese as a prophetic seed for the whole Body as they declared His supreme rule as King of kings and Lord of lords over His Bride, from every color and tribe and nation. Then Chuck Pierce, standing on behalf of the Western church leaders, presented a key, inscribed with Isaiah 22:22, to the leaders of the Mainland Chinese church. This was a prophetic symbol of the West acknowledging and affirming the role God is giving the Chinese to lead the next wave in the Church.

THE ROAD TO JERUSALEM

If we look at the bigger picture of the Church since Christ came to earth, we know that its foundations were laid by the Jewish people—the twelve apostles and faithful early converts. There were no Gentiles in the Church at this time.

But when the Lord opened the door for the Gentiles, it brought the Church into a whole new dimension of our journey; the phase of taking the gospel literally from Jerusalem to the ends of the earth. This phase, led primarily by the Western Church, has lasted almost two thousand years and was primarily evangelism- and missions-oriented. But the next and final stage of the Church, I believe, will be the Church returning from the ends of the earth to Jerusalem and it will lead to an unprecedented outpouring of the Holy Spirit and world-impacting revival.

Many people speak about the "back to Jerusalem" movement, and the Chinese Church has recognized this is a part of their destiny as a people. But what does this term "back to Jerusalem" actually mean? One view is that it's about preaching the gospel in the Middle East. And there is truth in this as we will always have a mandate to preach the gospel everywhere we go and to see the lost saved.

But I think there is another angle that we may not have fully understood. I believe that the Lord is also entrusting the Chinese to lead the nations into the convergence of the end-time Kingdom. What do I mean by that? The Church worldwide is going to make its way "back to Jerusalem" in the spirit realm, reclaiming all the Lord originally intended His Body to be. And through this journey, God will confront the principalities and powers that have kept the Church captive for centuries.

SHAKING THE IDOLS

The Kingdom of God was never meant to just be a teaching, it was meant to be the living reality of the Church. But in order for God to birth this unshakable Kingdom among and through the Body of Christ, first He must shake the kingdoms of this world and set the Church free from the powers that have defiled His name.

The financial meltdown that began on Rosh Hashanah 2008 and left the economies of many nations destabilized is a first sign of this shaking. God is determined to set His people free from the control of Mammon so that through the Church, He can birth a new economy based on His laws and principles. It will be the economy of the Josephs and the Daniels.

The increasing turmoil in the Middle East in the last few years is another major sign of the clash between kingdoms. Egypt is shaking and so are Iran, Iraq, Syria, and Turkey to name a few. Why? Because these are the nations that were the birthing places of many ancient strongholds, the habitations of powerful spirits that are still ruling in the earth today. And God is looking to confront these spirits, like the spirit of the prince of Persia and the Babylonian system which, fueled by the power of human initiative, seeks to build a name for itself. And He will also confront the spirit of religion that we see warring over the land of Israel, as well as the gods of Egypt.

Some people think the gods of Egypt are long gone. But they didn't vanish, they just took on new names in our modern culture—Freemasonry and the New Age. Both of these systems find their roots in Egypt. That's why the Freemasons have adopted the obelisk, the pyramid, and the "all-seeing eye." Have you ever wondered why many of the major financial centers of the world have an obelisk? It's because the Freemasons took them from Egypt and erected them in these places so that they could exert spiritual control over all the financial systems of the world.

Now in our Western rational mindset we think, "What are you talking about? An obelisk is just a statue. What kind of power is in a statue?" Well, if you want to know the power, go back to First Samuel 5 when the Ark of the Covenant went into the temple of the Philistines. There was a god in that temple in a statue form called Dagon. And when the Ark of the Covenant entered the temple of the Philistines, that statue, Dagon, fell down. Why would a statue fall down if it's just a rock? After all, a rock can't think or see. So why did it fall down? It fell because there was a spirit inhabiting that statue and in the presence of God, there is no power that can stand. So down Dagon went, bowing before the Ark. The next day the Philistines found him and pushed him back up. But when they returned, what did they find? Dagon was not only bowed down, now he was broken too.

Isaiah 19 is a prophecy about Egypt and the end times. And the first line of that prophecy says that the Lord is coming on a swift cloud and the idols of Egypt will tremble. And the ancient "gods of Egypt," these spirits that have tried to exercise their rule through governmental and financial authorities, are being shaken.

ESTABLISHING AN UNSHAKEABLE KINGDOM

But it is very important for us to remember that this battle, the clash of the kingdoms, is not something you and I can face on our own. This battle is the Lord's and all we need to do is align ourselves behind the Commander in Chief. God is looking for a people, a remnant from throughout the nations, over whom He can reign and rule. And the Lord will use humble, broken people who don't care about their reputation but only care about the Name of the Lord being honored and the Kingdom of God being established. And through these people, He will confront these spirits.

That's why I believe at this hour the Lord is calling the Church to another standard, because He wants to establish His Kingdom over our hearts. He wants to reign and rule in His Church. And for that to happen, we have to make the decision not to tolerate any more defilement in our lives. No more mixture in our hearts, no more mixture in our thoughts.

If you have been enduring a time of shaking in your life, don't be discouraged. This is the preparation of the Lord for you. He is shaking you not to destroy you but to prepare you for the unshakable. So count it all joy and don't look back. If you are alive in this hour, it is because the Lord has a purpose for you. You are called to be part of His overcoming Kingdom.

THE V-FORMATION

I believe that it is because of God's plan to establish His over-coming Kingdom that He has destined the Chinese to take the lead in this hour. The Chinese Church has been shaken, tested, and tried, even to the point of death. Yet they have remained steadfast and faithful, unswerving in their absolute devotion and surrender to the King. And as they have embraced humility and brokenness for His sake, now the Lord is raising them up with an authority to birth a pure seed of the establishment of the King-dom on behalf of the whole Body of Christ.

But that doesn't mean that the rest of us, especially those of us from the Western Church, can just sit back and watch them run. Often we have heard the moves of God described like a relay race—one runner finishes his leg and passes the baton on to the next. And this is a true picture when we are talking about one generation releasing the torch to the next generation as they pass away from the earth. But in the accelerated times in which we are living, we are not only seeing one move in a generation, we are seeing many. And so perhaps a better way of looking at these leadership transitions in the global Body is to look at the V-formation that is common among the Canadian geese. A whole flock of geese fly together, but there is one goose which is posi-tioned at the very front of the V, to take the full force of the wind resistance and make it easier for all those behind him. But of course, facing that wind is exhausting, so after a period of time the lead goose will move back into the formation while another goose will take his place at the head of the V.

And that's how I see what God is doing right now with the Chi-nese. For a long time, the Western Church has been positioned at the front of the V, leading the charge through many moves of God over centuries. And I believe the Lord is saying, "Western Church, you have done well and you have broken through again and again for the rest of the Church worldwide. But now I have specially prepared another part of My body, the Chinese, to take the lead for this leg of the journey. And they will have the faith and perseverance needed to stand strong in the face of the resistance that is coming."

This kind of shift in leadership takes a certain amount of humility and grace from both parties. First, the Western Church, which has been used to leading for a very long time, has to be willing to acknowledge the hand of God upon the Chinese. And we have to understand that, though our position may be changing, that doesn't mean that we can leave the flock. We need to remain in the formation, flying together, supporting the leadership of the Chinese. At the same time, the Chinese have to have the humility to honor what the Western Church has sown, because honoring the fathers, those who have gone before us, is what keeps us in the flow of continuous blessing of the Lord.

I have been genuinely touched to see how much God has deposited this heart to honor in the Chinese. When Chuck Pierce presented the key to the mainland Chinese leaders in August 2012, their response was to fall on their knees, thanking the Western Church for their sacrifice in sending missionaries, men like Hudson Taylor and thousands of others, who gave their lives to see God's purposes being fulfilled among the Chinese. They also repented for their historic sins of rejecting, persecuting, and even killing these missionaries. And then they declared something truly beautiful: "As God now gives us the privilege to lead, we will rise up and bring a fulfillment to everything the Western spiritual fathers and mothers had hoped for and longed to see." Then they turned to the Western Church leaders standing on stage with them and said, "Please walk with us. We need your wisdom, we need your support, and we need your love. We are one family."

GOD'S SOVEREIGN PLAN

So I believe God has uniquely positioned the Chinese, through their faithfulness and humility, to lead in the Church in this part of our end-time journey—from the ends of the earth back to Jerusalem. But the Chinese also possess a key, something beyond their freedom from the fear of death that qualifies them for this journey—an equally fervent love for the sons of Ishmael and for the sons of Isaac.

The Chinese Church loves the Jewish people in the same way that they love and feel called to the Arabs. And in His wisdom, God has even positioned the Chinese in the natural realm to have major favor among the Arabs as well as respect among the Jews. So the Chinese are able to go where the Western Church cannot. They are able to stretch their arms wide to embrace not only the sons of Ishmael and the sons of Isaac, but also the Western Church, bringing the whole Body together into one family.

THE RESTORATION OF ALL THINGS

Acts 3:21 tells us that a time is coming before the return of Jesus when the Father will restore everything. Every promise will be fulfilled, including the one spoken in Haggai 2:9: "The glory of this present house will be greater than the glory of the former house." I believe one of the next major restorations we are going to witness as the Body of Christ heads "back to Jerusalem" will be the fulfillment of the Feast of Tabernacles—God dwelling among His people in a way unprecedented since the days of Solomon.

I can see how again, in His sovereign wisdom and timing, the Lord is raising up the Chinese to be forerunners in this for the whole global Body of Christ. What I am witnessing today among the Chinese defies description. Their humility and complete abandonment to the will of God is allowing the Lord to speedily bring them into unity one with another and alignment with His headship. And the presence of God that I have experienced when I am among the Chinese, I believe, is a foretaste of the glory that is the Bride's inheritance in the last days. And I trust the Lord will use this deposit of His presence among the Chinese to provoke jealousy in the rest of the Church, causing a remnant in every nation to begin to cry out to the Lord to prepare them also to be a resting place for His glory.

WISE MEN FROM THE EAST

Two thousand years ago, wise men from the East followed the signs pointing to the coming Messiah. Today, as part of their eternal destiny, the Lord is once again raising up "wise men from the East" as forerunners to trumpet a call to the Church world-wide to recognize the signs of her soon-returning King.

In the global "chess board" of God's end-time purposes, the Lord is now surprising His opponent by moving His "Chinese piece" into a strategic position, a spiritual "checkmate" that will assure His victory at the end of the game.

To the Chinese believers—the Spirit is calling you to embrace your destiny. You have been brought into the Kingdom for such a time as this.

To all the Asian brethren—the time has come for "wise men from the East" to walk in humility and brokenness together as one so that you might to fulfill your mandate to awaken the global Body to the hour in which we are living.

And to the Western Church—God is asking you by faith and humility to join with the Chinese believers as they lead the whole Body of Christ in this new journey, from the ends of the earth back to Jerusalem.

May God grant the grace for us all to walk together as one man in complete submission to the headship of Christ, bringing pleasure to the heart of the Father and the fulfillment of His pur-poses for the Bride worldwide.

For almost fifteen years, under the umbrella of Watchmen for the Nations (a relational network of hundreds of ministries in Canada), David facilitated a journey among a remnant of the Canadian church to stand in the gap to redeem the destiny of the nation. He began traveling to China in 2006 after a group of leaders, who had attended a Canadian national gathering, shared their longing to see the Chinese walk in the same redemptive journey for their people that they had experienced in Canada. Today David's main focus is walking with leaders in China and other Asian countries, helping them to facilitate their own journeys to see the redemptive destinies of their nations released and the Bride of Christ prepared for Jesus's return.

For more information about David and the journey among the Chinese and Asian nations, please visit www .asiagathering.hk.

CHAPTER 10

THE GREAT, GREATER AWAKENING

Julie Meyer

I SAW:

God is stirring His people to pray. God is raising up houses of prayer, prayer movements, and ministries who realize the great need for prayer and have a foundation of intercession firmly established before ministry takes place; people are bowing their knees in reverence to our Holy God, believing that He gives more when we simply ask. God set it up that way, that we would be co-laborers with Him, joining Jesus, the Great Intercessor, and simply asking—knowing that God is listening and answering our simple prayers (see Isa. 64:4).

The revivalists of old were men and women given to prayer. Before a word was preached, the heavens were stormed with prayers and petitions asking God to come, to act, and to move. We are entering a new era, for never before in history has God moved on the hearts of people worldwide with an invitation to intercession. For across the nations of the earth, men and women, young and old are giving their lives as a fragrance before the Lord in day and night prayer. Houses of prayer, prayer movements, and praying churches are arising worldwide with the revelation that God moves when His people simply ask.

I heard a fresh cry exploding out of heaven, an invitation for the nations to become part of the prayer movement that is blowing across the face of the earth like an unstoppable wave leading to a great, greater awakening. I was told in the dream to study and look back to the 1700s and the First Great Awakening, for this is our story. We are invited to say *yes* to prayer; we are invited to all become part of the story. I saw many intercessors have grown weary and become dull. Therefore help from heaven was sent to strengthen the heart of the intercessor, the prayer movements, and the houses of prayer so that a glorious people would arise in unending prayers.

We are in a Revelation 3 timeframe: "I know your works, that you have a name that you are alive, but you are dead. Be watchful, and strengthen the things which remain…" (Rev. 3:1-2 NKJV).

God is inviting us to join His Son, the Great Intercessor, in prayer, to birth His purposes on the earth. He is inviting us to be a part of the story line of the ages, to be vigilant, to keep careful watch over His promises and purposes through intercession, to set our hearts toward Him, to turn resolutely in the direction of agreement with His heart for these days.

I HAD A DREAM:

I was in a deep sleep and dreamt that I was awakened by the president of our Bible college singing an old hymn called "I Love to Tell the Story." His voice was like a megaphone awakening my heart to the old, old story. I had not heard this hymn in years since singing it as a young girl in the Methodist church. He was wearing a blue suit and holding an old hymnal. His voice was loud. His voice was strong. He never stopped singing this song, this old hymn throughout the entire dream. As he was singing this song, these words and the melody awakened my heart all throughout the dream. It was as if the backdrop to the entire dream was the old hymn.

Suddenly, I stepped into a scene where I saw seven ambulances all in a row and with their lights flashing. They were lined up one in back of the other. There was great alarm in my spirit when my eyes beheld such a scene.

I noticed there were people on the sidewalk who were not that interested in the ambulances as everyone was continuing to have coffee and talk—they were not looking at what was happening. The people were just doing their thing, not bothered by these flashing lights, not bothered by the alarm that I felt in my body by the flashing lights. It was as if they did not even notice they were there. They were laughing and talking and having coffee, going about their day-to-day schedules.

Still the song was arising:

> I love to tell the story.
> Twill be my theme in glory.
> To tell the old, old story
> Of Jesus and His love.

I went and looked in the first ambulance and I heard the attendant say, "I cannot find a heartbeat." I saw someone lying still on a gurney. I saw tiny, thin, feeble legs. The attendant looked at me and said, "It's the intercessors. We are trying to revive the intercessors." I looked in again and it was as if the eyes of my heart were opened and I could see on the inside and their hearts were failing. For the promises of revival were so long in coming, it was as if the promises became too long to wait for and they were giving up and their hearts were failing.

So I ran to the next ambulance and the same thing was happening. I looked in and the attendant said, "I cannot find a heartbeat."

As I peered into the ambulance, I noticed that these attendants were not mere human beings, they were heavenly beings sent from the Throne of God. They were tall, they were large, they were glowing as if lit from the inside with fire. Could these be the messengers of fire we find in Psalms 104:4? It gave my heart great hope to know that God has sent His angelic help to restart the hearts of the weary, the tired, the hopeless, the feeble—these were the intercessors who have fallen asleep, those who have stopped contending because it became too long to contend.

Suddenly, one of the attendants from the seventh ambulance at the end yelled, "I have a faint heartbeat, but it's dull." With those words, all the attendants leaned out of the back doors of the ambulances and they all shouted, "What did you do?"

The attendant in the last ambulance said, "Tell the old, old stories. For, as I began to tell the old, old stories, I found a faint heartbeat." So the attendants of the other ambulances began to tell the old, old stories, and I began to listen to these stories.

These stories went back to the 1700s. They began to talk about Count Zinzendorf and the Moravians, John Wesley, George Whitfield, and Charles Spurgeon. Suddenly, the atmosphere was filled with shouts: "I found a heartbeat, but it is dull."

I ran to another ambulance and looked in, but this time I saw a faint movement. Suddenly, this heavenly attendant gave an order like a command, saying:

> Tell the old, old stories; because the old, old stories are *your* story line, they are *your* history, back as far as Count Zinzendorf and the Moravians, John Wesley, George Whitfield, Charles Spurgeon. For as the baton was passed from generation to generation, the prayer movements of this day are the answer to the prayers of those in the great story line of the ages. There is a timeline of prayer generals from generations past, and their prayer was that the generals of prayer in "these" days would arise; for the prayer movement of "these" days is the answer to their cries. You are in the story line of the old, old story, for their prayers begat your prayer.

Put yourself in the timeline of the old, old story, because the old, old story, when told, will ignite the heart again. Though it will start as a dull beat, when *each* person will see themselves in the timeline of the old, old story, that dull heartbeat will began to get stronger and stronger. For these are your ancestors—the prayer warriors of the ancient days—who lifted their cry for "this day and this hour," that a people of prayer would arise in the earth to welcome back the King of kings.

Renewal in itself will not awaken dull hearts, but the more you listen and put yourself in the history of the great story line of prayer and revival—in the midst of the old, old story—the more you see yourself as *the answer.* You are the continuation of their prayers. For the intercessors God is raising up today, the prayer movements in the earth today, are the answer to the prayers lifted up generations and generations ago, taking us into the greatest awakening—the Great, Greater Awakening.

These are your ancestors. *You* become the story, the plan, the answer, the revival for today. Then you will never go back to dull hearts.

And the attendant said again and again:

Tell the old, old stories. Remember the old, old stories and see yourself in the story line of Count Zinzendorf and the Moravians, John Wesley, George Whitfield and Charles Spurgeon, and many others who were great men and women of prayer—Charles Finney, Maria Woodworth-Etter, Smith Wigglesworth, Aimee Semple McPherson, Kathryn Kuhlman.

You are *in* their story, their history in *your* history, for you are the answer to their prayers that a glorious praying people who love prayer, a shining and praying Bride would arise in the earth. And this cry of prayer will birth the Great, Greater Awakening to welcome Him back.

And still I could hear the song being sung:

I love to tell the story of unseen things above,
Of Jesus and His glory, of Jesus and His love.
I love to tell the story, because I know 'tis true;
It satisfies my longings as nothing else can do.

I love to tell the story, 'twill be my theme in glory,
To tell the old, old story of Jesus and His love.

I love to tell the story; more wonderful it seems
Than all the golden fancies of all our golden dreams.
I love to tell the story, it did so much for me;
And that is just the reason I tell it now to thee.

I love to tell the story; 'tis pleasant to repeat
What seems, each time I tell it, more wonderfully sweet.
I love to tell the story, for some have never heard
The message of salvation from God's own holy Word.

I love to tell the story, for those who know it best
Seem hungering and thirsting to hear it like the rest.
And when, in scenes of glory, I sing the new, new song,
'Twill be the old, old story that I have loved so long.

THAT WAS THE DREAM

It was almost as if I could hear prayers that were prayed centuries back, even by John Wesley, crying out for those who would take the baton to begin to cry out again until the coming of the Lord Jesus Christ. You are a part of the story; we are a part of the story. It is almost as if we are the answer to the cries of prayer throughout the ages.

Cries that said, "Let a people who love prayer welcome Him back; let a praying people lift their voice for revival; let a billion souls come into the Kingdom."

This is our story. This is our history. This is our season to take the baton and pray and watch revival spring up. We are in their story line and they are in ours.

Aimee Semple McPherson's life was marked by unprecedented boldness, saying, "Let's not waste our time quarreling over methods and doctrines." She accomplished what no man had been able to do and built a temple that seated 5,000 people and filled it four times on Sundays and twice weekly, and this temple became the envy of Hollywood theater owners. She also ministered at highly sought-after healing services. She reached the unreachable and opened doors for Christ which no man had done before through media. It is interesting to note that in the same year Aimee was launching her radio station, Kathryn Kuhlman was just beginning to preach as a teenager, and Maria Woodworth-Etter had just breathed her last breath at 80 years of age.

This is our story. This is *our* history. Through prayer we put ourselves in the story line of the ages to welcome the Great, Greater Awakening.

Julie Meyer is a longtime and beloved worship leader and songwriter at the International House of Prayer in Kansas City since its beginning in 1999. She is a prophetic singer who carries the glory and the presence of God as an abandoned worshiper. Her passion is His presence as she trumpets the message of the Bridegroom preparing His Bride. She has lead worship and spoken worldwide on hearing the voice of God, prophetic singing, and worship. www.juliemeyer.com

CHAPTER 11

THE PROPHESIED HOUR OF A HOLY GENERATION

by Shawn Bolz

God is doing something amazing in this generation. There is an expansion in the heart of this very generation involving a unique destiny. It is not just that a few people are called in a special way, but the whole generation is burning with purpose. I want to share a portion of my personal testimony that I walked out in a prophetic journey.

When I was fifteen years old a prophetic friend by the name of Theresa Lea moved to our church. She prophesied over me that I would meet a prophet named Bob Jones who would come into my life, and when he did my whole commission for ministry would start with the higher purposes of my calling and destiny. I knew of Bob and he had even prayed for me at a conference once before, but I had not been around him for many years. I wanted to seek him out but I knew I needed to wait on the sovereignty of God or else it would be human effort and God would not get the maximum glory He desired.

After a few years went by I asked my friend, "Theresa, it has been five years, are you sure about your prophetic word involving Bob Jones?" I seemed so far from meeting him. We were not even in ministry circles that related to each other much, but I loved him in my heart.

She responded "You will meet him before the year 2003." That seemed like an eternity away in 1998 when she said it, so I just let it go although it was always in my heart; historically Theresa has been such an accurate voice and a lover of God, I knew it had the earmark of reality in it.

Well into the midnight hour of the word, November of 2002, Paul Keith and Wanda Davis paid my way to go to a conference in Albany, Oregon. We had met the previous month at a conference and they felt like I was supposed to come to Albany because it was going to be significant. They are like family with Bob Jones, and the Lord had told them that I was supposed to meet him and the rest of their team. (They didn't know my word and they invited me, which I thought was exciting.) I knew this was God and was amazed because it was one month from 2003! What an awesome fulfillment!

THE SPIRIT OF HEROD KILLING A GENERATION

The first night that I arrived in Albany, we all went to dinner and Bob prophesied over me for a long while. He started: "I prophesied four years before abortion was legalized that the spirit of Herod was attacking a generation and was going to try and take out a whole generation of anointed leaders by legalizing abortion. I prophesied it again in 1973 that God was going to raise up the generation in 30 years that the enemy was targeting for destruction. Just like the same enemy tried to take out Moses and then Jesus."

He asked me, "When were you born?" I told him April 26, 1974. He smiled and said, 'That means you were conceived in 1973, the very year that abortion was legalized, and you are one of those the enemy wanted to take out. Now that it is almost thirty years later, you are going to come into the very purpose of what you were created for. Your thirtieth birthday will be a key time." I had a profound sense of destiny for our entire generation because of what the enemy had tried to rob us of by taking out so many.

Bob continued, "I also prophesied back then that there would be a partial reversing of the abortion law in January of 2003. It will happen." In January of 2003, just as Bob had seen, President Bush revoked partial-birth abortions in our nation. It was the 30th anniversary of legalized abortion in our country. God has brought numerous profound signs in our generation for who we are called to be and the seriousness of the day in which we are living.

The next day, November 21, 2002, after meeting Bob Jones, I had a spiritual experience while in the hotel room in Albany.

SPIRITUAL VISION AND EXPERIENCE OF ISAIAH 22:22

In the experience, I was in a heavenly vision and an angel who was sent to bring me to a higher place in heaven came to me. He said to me, "Come, let us go to the prophet's house." I was in awe because I was in heaven going to a prophet's house! I wondered who it would be! He led me to an estate and we were on the outside of two enormous gates. They were golden gates that had words inscribed all through the bars. Beyond the gates there was a huge cloud of swirling light, color, and sound. I could barely see the actual house because of this, and I had no idea what I was really seeing because it was so awesome to me.

"This is the prophet's house, and it has been locked up for a very long time." He looked at me and I felt great respect for him. He continued, "But I have the key to open the gates," he showed me a large golden key, "and I am going to open them on November 22, 2002."

I said, "But that's tomorrow!" He smiled at me and I knew it was a parable because he didn't explain it. I was going to have to find the hidden meaning later. "Whose house is this?" I asked, "Which prophet?"

"Isaiah has been locked in his chambers for a long time," was his response. I pictured him in there reading ancient books. I was given spiritual understanding that some of the promises of Isaiah were about to be released upon the earth, and when I came out of the experience I began to ponder its meaning.

As I talked to a friend of mine about this, we began asking God, "What passage in Isaiah are you highlighting?" and immediately I saw a calendar in front of me in an open vision. It pointed to a day, then that day came in front of me: November 22, 2002. Then I saw November and the two zeros go away and it read: 22, 22. I knew the Lord was speaking to me so we looked it up in the Bible. This is what we found.

In Isaiah 22, there was a man by the name of Shebna who was in charge of the palace of the king. He was an elder in Israel and he was wrongly using the riches of the palace by stealing for his own gain. This was a serious offense to the Lord because it was such a key position over the treasuries of God. The Lord rebuked him and took him out of his position because of this and appointed a young man named Eliakim, which means "God of raising." God is "raising" up a generation of Eliakims where many in the church have been like Shebna.

Shebna prostituted his position, using for personal gain the very leadership role that the Lord had appointed him to, which was holy. Eliakim was believed to be a young man, maybe not even of the age of an elder yet, but he was given the position by the Lord over the treasury of the kingdom. It was demanded of Shebna to give all of his authority over to Eliakim, which was a great dishonor to Shebna because of Eliakim's age and the fact that he was from a lesser family. Then the Lord told Eliakim an amazing thing:

I will place on his shoulder the key to the house of David; what he opens no one can shut, and what he shuts no one can open (Isaiah 22:22).

This is the generation God is raising up right now—a generation with a double portion. It will be a generation that carries a 22-pound heart—a heart that Isaiah 22:22 is written upon—that they can open a door that no man has ever opened to usher in the kingdom age of God! Also a generation that can shut a door to the old forms of religious expression that no longer are relevant—old wineskins, that no man will ever be able to resurrect with any anointing! After getting understanding into this experience, I had two more visions.

VISION OF THE STAR FALLING

Immediately following this experience, I saw a star falling; it seemed like the brightest star in the universe. I heard the voice of the Lord internally, audibly proclaim out of Isaiah 14:12, "How you have fallen from heaven, morning star, son of the dawn!" This speaks about Satan falling from his high position in the heavens. The Lord spoke to me and said, "The spirit of Herod has fallen from this generation! No longer will the persecution from the enemy be greater than the release of My Spirit in churches, cities, and countries." I remembered Bob Jones's word to our generation: Just like Herod tried to abort the promised child of Israel, there is a spirit like Herod that has been warring against this generation, trying to take out anointed deliverers, and his power is no more!

I heard the voice of the Lord: "How you have fallen, oh Spirit of Herod."

Then I saw a generation looking at this spirit saying, "Is this the one who killed so many of us, who tried to abort our purpose? The one who had us trapped in the desert, who overthrew the justice of God in our nations and who brought us into captivity?"

He had no more power compared to the power that God was offering this generation!

OPEN VISION OF AN ANGEL AND THE PEG

Right after that vision I was hit on the head by something in the natural. I opened my eyes and an angel was flying by in my hotel room holding a peg, like a railroad spike or large wooden stake. I immediately went into intercession for my grandfather. His name is Ozzy Osborne (he is not the rock singer). He and my step-grandmother have been leaders in the occult for many years and are recognized as leading spiritualists. They are a part of an organization that trains people how to hear spirits and heal the sick through these false spiritual powers. As I was praying for him I realized that his life was being sustained by demonic powers. He was old and had several heart attacks but still miraculously lived. The Lord gave me a promise when I was in my teens that He would visit Ozzy before he died, giving him mercy if Ozzy would accept Him.

As I was interceding, I heard the voice of the Lord say, "I am removing your grandfather, who has been a curse to you and your family." I realized it was out of the passage of Isaiah 22:25 and symbolically the angel that had just flown by had taken out the peg that was driven into the firm place (Shebna's support) so that the new peg could be driven in (Eliakim).

I heard the Lord again: "I am removing your grandfather from your family as a sign that every obstacle that has been in the way of your generation from entering into its fullness would be removed. Just as the spirit of Herod's power has been removed, your grandfather represents influence of that power and is being removed so that there can be a calling forth of spiritual heritage."

I told my friends Paul Keith and Wanda Davis this after the experience. The very next day, on November 22, 2002, my grandfather died in his sleep.

God is serious about what He is willing to do for this generation to be given an expansion from heaven to carry His heart to the ends of the earth. He will let nothing stop us from His goal.

Heidi Baker is a woman of God who ministers in Mozambique, Africa. Our team recently was able to minister with her at a conference in Red Deer, Canada. She shared an experience she had. It was a powerful heavenly experience in which she saw a line of chariots coming down from heaven from the throne of God where Jesus was. There were two transparent riders per chariot, and they each had a humongous heart inside their chest that went from shoulder to shoulder—an enlarged heart!

She was also able to see inside the breast of Jesus as well and His heart was a shoulder-to-shoulder heart. It was beating intensely, and as she looked at those riding on the chariots, she saw that their hearts were beating in perfect cadence with the heart of Jesus! It was a holy rhythm of heart beating; representing that these riding upon the chariots were moving in the clouds of Heaven to represent the moves of God that will be in perfect sync with the very heart of Jesus.

This is what the generation of the 22-pound heart will look like—those who ride upon the wings of the wind, in sync with the very desire of Jesus. Chariots represent vehicles of ministry from heaven being released upon the earth that will carry a supernatural stewardship of love that will birth signs and wonders, healings, and a prophetic anointing.

Much has been invested in this multi-generational plan of heaven to demonstrate the power and glory of Jesus in this day. Our adversary has fought diligently to eradicate a generation in hopes of frustrating the plan of God. However, the Lord will have His day and a body of radical warriors who possess the hearts of champions that beat in perfect unison with His.

THE PROPHESIED HOUR OF A HOLY GENERATION

In the past several months, there has been even more unfolding to our understanding of the times and seasons we are living in. We wanted to continue building a prophetic perspective with revelations to inspire a generation to apprehend her mandate for this hour.

THE ROOM OF THE ABORTED

In heaven, there is a special room that a few prophetic people have seen through visions and trances. I saw it first when I was sixteen years old and it helped me to understand God's justice system. Recently I saw this spiritual place again and discovered it is a room within the courts of heaven. It is called the "abortion room," and in this room there are millions of innocents who were destroyed through abortion before their purpose on earth could be completed.

These precious ones are crying out before the Mercy Seat. They long for a recompense to be delivered to Jesus in response to their lives being cut short.

I heard the cry of one of the females who was aborted, and she was pointing down at a girl her exact same age on the earth who was still alive. "Lord, You know that I was killed and my calling was aborted, not just my life; will You expand her calling (finger-pointing the young lady on earth) and give her my purpose that You had created for me before the beginning of time so that You can inherit Your full reward?" To this God said yes, and the girl on earth was expanded supernaturally to walk in more anointing and purpose than she would ever be able to accomplish by her own calling.

I began to hear a roar of those in this "abortion room" in heaven as they shouted forth their similar requests, pointing to those who were on the earth and appealing to God to release their callings upon a generation. I could see people who were in this generation receiving as many as seven callings from those who were in heaven petitioning their God. How is God going to inherit the earth through a generation? We need to begin to understand how the justice of God works—a sevenfold anointing is being released!

> *Yet if he* [the thief] *is caught, he must pay sevenfold, though it costs him all the wealth of his house* (Proverbs 6:31).

ONE BILLION IN ONE GENERATION!

When God prophetically told Bob Jones about the abortion issues more than 30 years ago, he also heard from the Lord that there would be an abortion pill that women would take to kill their unborn babies. In 1973, that seemed unlikely to the people who heard Bob. People believed him to be way off-base from the truth.

One day Satan came to Bob and threatened, "If you continue to speak this message, I will kill you!" Bob knew that if he didn't speak the message, God would kill him, so he kept speaking. In 1975, Bob was in his home and had an attack that came on his body and he died. His heavenly report is awesome. During it God told Bob, face to face, that He was going to save one billion souls in one generation, and it would be a youth movement. Interestingly, there are over seven billion people on the earth, and the secular statistics state that over half of the people alive right now are under the age of 18.

THE SON'S PASSION IS FLARING TOWARD US

Recently Bob prophesied that there would be a sign in the sun. He told us and a group of young people, "Watch the sun for a sign." Amazingly a solar flare that is two times as big as any that has ever hit the earth was released toward us. This happened just days before President Bush signed the bill that revoked partial-birth abortion. Even though this legislative bill needs more done before it is pushed completely through, God is using it as a sign of the times to state the release of this generation into its holy purpose.

Secular scientists have diagrammed the sun into sections and this solar flare came from section 486. For those of you who do not know, the abortion pill that Bob Jones had prophesied came out in the 1980s and was called RU486!

We were stunned when the solar flare came from that section of the sun toward the earth. When the gasses from the solar flare hit our earth, some scientists predicted minimal effects from it. Nonetheless, these gasses were literally absorbed into our atmosphere and we believe will have affect on the earth including adverse weather patterns and the earth's electromagnetic fields.

THE SUN OF RIGHTEOUSNESS

I believe that the Son's passion and justice has flared toward us. Just like the natural sun is a signpost, the atmosphere of the heavenly Son is on its way toward us:

> *"Surely the day is coming; it will burn like a furnace. All the arrogant and every evildoer will be stubble, and that day that is coming will set them on fire," says the Lord Almighty. "Not a root or a branch will be left to them. But for you who revere my name, the sun of righteousness will rise with healing in its rays. And you will go out and frolic like well-fed calves. Then you will trample on the wicked; they will be ashes under the soles of your feet on the day when I act," says the Lord Almighty* (Malachi 4:1-3).

In Malachi 4:2, it literally uses the analogy of the sun rising upon us with healing for us birthed out of His great righteousness. This is a messianic picture that I believe we can apply to this very season we are in; the sign given from our sun points to the great love of a jealous God, the Lord Jesus Christ.

This is a truly divine hour we are living in and the purpose of God is being released toward us in unprecedented ways. This statement can be taken as hype or exaggeration, or we can see that God is using signs in this day to confirm His purpose and word that He is pursuing a whole generation with justice, but through passion.

SOWING INTO THE YOUNGER GENERATION

Through many of my writings I have written numerous articles involving the younger generation. I am not considered a youth leader or young adult minister. However, the Lord has often encountered me as an "older" one of the younger generation who has grown up with purpose and destiny as part of Joel's army.

Our ministry loves and is called to equip people of all age groups. We as an entire generation are about to enter one of the greatest spiritual purposes in history. Theresa Lea, a good friend of ours and a powerfully anointed prophetic person, has often said, "We must see each other at the end of the race holding a trophy."

Bob Jones, one of our mentors and friends, goes so far as to say that his ceiling must become our floor. That is the mentality of our training, to allow people to walk on our experience, not come up under it. While at a wonderful conference held by Frontline Worship Center in Alberta, Canada, this phrase took on significant meaning. During a session conducted by Heidi Baker, I went into a spiritual trance that transitioned into an open vision. The vision revealed many young people on the earth right now. I saw that God had made an investment into them and that it was time to harvest this investment; it was a fullness of time moment. The revelation seemed to emphasize people who were young adults, though every age group will be vital in God's plan.

As I observed this future army, there was not much about them that seemed compelling. Suddenly the Holy Spirit began to hover over them and my eyes were opened to see them from God's perspective. The young people in front of me were transformed as though they were at the end of their lives having finished their race as champions; each one was holding the victor's trophy. It was amazing because as I looked at each one of them, my spiritual eyes were opened to see the fullness of what was available to them. I could see their opportunities for greatness and the ability offered them to find Jesus in a way that was rare and awesome.

EYES OF ETERNITY

"This is how I see them," The Holy Spirit said to me, "I see them at the end of their race with the trophy in hand."

I remembered Theresa's voice saying these same words. I looked again and I saw them normal; the glory had faded. They were in the same condition as when the vision started; they were not visibly special. They were no longer in their fullness as I had seen them spiritually. They were just irresponsible young people who seemed more self-absorbed than any generation before.

"What do you see in front of you?" the Lord asked.

"I don't want to tell You; I liked what I saw a moment ago when they had their trophies and crowns," I responded.

The Lord then said, "That is how I always see them. I want to invite you to see them in their fullness, at the end of the race, fully rewarded for their 'yes' to Me. If you see them this way with My eyes then you will treat them this way. If you treat them this way, then they can rise up to the occasion to run the race of life as overcomers. They will rise up and live after the spiritual truth that you awaken and invite them to."

The Lord then revealed John in the book of Revelation chapters 2 and 3 when He spoke to him about the seven churches. Jesus was very honest with their weaknesses but invited them into His fullness. He promised them many things based on His expectation that they would desire to say "yes" to His Spirit who would empower them to "overcome." The key is that He didn't hope they would; He knew already the ones whose desire was for Him. To them He imparted the virtue to overcome.

JOHN'S GREAT REVELATION OF THE FULLY PREPARED BRIDE

I then saw John in Revelation 19 as he was given the vision of the radiant Bride who had embraced the righteousness of Christ. Obviously the whole Bride of Christ is not yet perfected, but John saw her as though she was. It was the most sacred thing that John saw besides Jesus Himself. Because of this, John was able to love those God loved on earth in a supernatural way because he saw them in the Lord's perfection. He saw her at the end of the race fully prepared as a Bride to meet her Bridegroom and say *"yes"* with all her heart.

This is the same principle that God desires that we use in looking at the younger generation. Not necessarily who they now are but who they can be. Many people are aware of their calling to invest into the younger generation but oftentimes do not know how. I challenge you to see them with the eyes of heaven from God's perspective in eternity. This will cause you to help them go higher toward their eternal destiny, not just treat them based on their current level of maturity (or lack thereof).

God is calling forth a generation that will advance in a Kingdom way. A paraphrased definition of growth in Kingdom principles involves maturing at an escalated pace. The speed of eternity is even faster than the speed of light. What takes 20 years for previous generations to learn becomes common for a

Kingdom generation to gain in only one year. Peter understood this principle in Second Peter 3:8.

In light of these revelations, we wanted to honor the vision by investing into the younger generation of leaders. They are the ones who may not even know what they are called to, but can feel the serious tug of eternity upon their destiny. I oversee Expression58 internship programs in fulfillment of a vision that the Lord birthed in me to train young people. It is designed for ages 17 to 25 (sometimes a little younger or older are included). The disciples who were on the road to Emmaus didn't initially know it was Jesus who was with them causing their hearts to burn within them, but when they found out they were never the same. They always had anticipation of encountering Him again in real ways and they never felt alone or without direction again. They maintained a place of conviction built both by the Word and their spiritual experience.

I believe this story is a parable of what God is doing in this generation. He is causing hearts to burn within us, and then revealing Himself to us. We want to encounter Jesus together this way and discover all the burning passions that He has inspired us with. In this internship, the young people live together, eat together, and press in to worship and intercession together; they will travel on ministry trips with Expression58 teams and partici-pate as part of the ministry team; get exposed to some serious mothers and fathers of the faith who also burn with passion; and basically see God in themselves in a way that will cause them to never look at anything but heaven as a goal.

Shawn Bolz founded Expression58, a missions base and church focused on training and equipping, the creative arts, the poor, and loving people in the entertainment industry. The base is now located in Los Angeles, California.

Shawn has written three books: *The Throne Room Company, Keys to Heavens Economy: An Angelic Visitation from the Minister of Finance,* and *The Nonreligious Guide to Dating and Being Single.* www.expression58.org

PART 3

HOW TO CHANGE THE WORLD

CHAPTER 12

YOUR ROLE IN THE DAYS TO COME

by Julia Loren

My dear brothers and sisters, my dearest daughters and sons, the future belongs to you. You have a distinct role in shaping how time unfolds. Nothing about your life and the world around you is written in stone.

All the prophecies of the ages reveal the coming Messiah and herald tumultuous times ahead of us. Every generation sees both horrible and wonderful things unfolding during their lifetime. We are no different. We have no idea when Jesus and the coming Kingdom will manifest so openly to all the world that we will behold Him and be with Him forever, as the ancient prophets foretold. What we do know is that you and I have been born into an amazing world and God knows the times and the seasons of our lives. We have been born for purpose, given amazing gifts and talents for a purpose—to glorify God and enjoy life to the fullest.

I believe that the happiest people on earth are those who have pursued their strengths and gifts and discovered how to use them to benefit the world. Finding meaning in your life and living out that meaning creates a future that is fulfilling to you and makes its mark on the world. We are meant to shape the history of our families and our world.

The future of us depends on the choices and responses you make today.

In my work as a writer and a life coach, many people come to me with their unformed gifts and broken dreams, feeling stuck from reaching their God-ordained potential, feeling like their life doesn't have much meaning. They wonder how to move out of the hindering past and into the freedom of tomorrow.

I encourage them to begin with refocusing on the goodness of God. The wrong concept of God and religion overburdens them with ideas of what they should be doing or guilt over what they have done or left undone. Their concept of the personality and nature of God becomes so warped that they no longer enjoy His presence. God loves to reveal Himself to hearts that are open to the Holy Spirit breathing new love and life into them.

It takes a listening heart, leaning into the voice of the Lord, interacting with Him through prayer and worship, to uncover who they are meant to be at this age and stage of life. Our gifts and talents change over time. Some gifts and anointings are more in use while you are young. Other gifts and anointings manifest more fully with age. There is no such thing as a dry and withered Christian destined for the sidelines when they reach the age of 50 or 65. We all have a purpose for being alive right now, today.

Part of that purpose involves intercessory prayer that births the plans and purposes of God into the world. This is one of the most important gifts and purposes that can unfold at any age. No matter what your state of health or mobility, God is calling you to partner with Him in prayer to release His plans and purposes throughout the world. The most revolutionary thing you can do in life is to release heaven's plans on earth through your prayers and prayer gatherings.

Part of your purpose also involves intercessory action— using your gifts and talents in whatever sphere of influence God is giving you. If you have an anointing for business, why seek to become a pastor of a church? If you are anointed for politics, why seek to become an educator? If you have a gift for the stock market, why seek someplace other than Wall Street? If you are a musician, writer, or artist, why seek to limit your audience to the Christian market and other believers?

Those who seek Jesus will find Him. Those who ask for wisdom and strategy will receive it. It is His promise to us. If you want to shape how the rest of your life will unfold and make a difference in the future of us, it is imperative that you seek Him and ask for wisdom and strategy. It is imperative that you discover your sacred destiny and walk in it.

The future belongs to you. What in you is waiting to be unleashed? What is your role in the days to come, a role that helps shape the future of the world?

SHAPING HISTORY THROUGH INTERCESSORY PRAYER

Through the centuries, great prayer movements have launched individuals into intercessory actions that changed political, economic, and social policies. Those prayer movements created an atmosphere that opened the heavens and released the Holy Spirit to move freely in their midst. E.M. Bounds, a Methodist pastor, wrote several enduring books on the subject of prayer and has witnessed the impact of prayer in his lifetime. According to Bounds, "Prayer, like faith, obtains promises, enlarges their operation, and adds to the measure of their results."

Many prayer movements have marked the greatest epochs in the growth of the Christian faith and in societal transformation. The church was born in a 24/7 prayer room in Jerusalem on the day of Pentecost, and it was said of them, "they all joined together constantly in prayer" (Acts 1:14).

Early Christianity was incubated by the monastic prayer centers of the desert fathers, the Celtic communities of Northern Europe, and eventually the Benedictine and other orders.

In the 18th century, a Moravian community, under the leadership of Count Zinzendorf, prayed night and day for more than a hundred years, thereby launching the great missionary thrust of the Reformation. One of their converts was John Wesley, founder of Methodism.

In the 20th century, a multi-racial 24/7 prayer room on Azusa Street in Los Angeles sparked the Pentecostal and charismatic movements, bringing spiritual renewal to nearly 500 million people today.

In our time, prayer movements are still shifting atmospheres and the hearts of believers and unbelievers around the world in many of the upper echelons of society. You are invited to take part in a prayer movement and shape how history unfolds. Many local churches sponsor unified prayer gatherings. Many apostolic centers also sponsor prayer gatherings and conferences. Some regions have prayer centers such as Chuck Pierce's Global Spheres Center in Denton, Texas that also houses the Israel Prayer Garden (www.gloryofzion.org). Colorado Springs World Prayer Center (www.theworldprayercenter.org) also offers prayer conferences and space to pray. Prayer Mountain, a Christian retreat in South Korea, operated by the Yoido Full Gospel Church, Korea's largest church (www.fgtv.com/n_english/prayer/p_index.asp), has been well-known for decades as a leading force in transforming the Korean Church and shaping culture.

Go! Join with others in prayer and watch what happens. Your voice is power. And when believers come together in unity, the presence of God moves.

Here are a few other connections offering opportunities for you to take part in this great groundswell of unified prayer rising up to shape history.

IHOP

Today, we have such movements as the Kansas City-based International House of Prayer (www.ihopkc.org) under Mike Bickle's leadership, drawing people into 24/7 prayer and worship.

On May 7, 1999, the International House of Prayer of Kansas City was founded by Mike Bickle and twenty full-time "intercessory missionaries," who cried out to God in prayer with worship for thirteen hours each day. Four months later, on September 19, 1999, prayer and worship extended to the full 24/7 schedule.

The International House of Prayer is an evangelical missions organization that is committed to praying for the release of the fullness of God's power and purpose, as we actively win the lost, heal the sick, feed the poor, make disciples, and impact every sphere of society—family, education, government, economy, arts, media, religion, etc.

People from all over the world come to IHOP to take part in the "Harp and Bowl" method of prayer that combines prayer and live instrumental worship. As a result, mini-IHOPs have sprung up around the nation, giving regional opportunities to join with others in prayer and worship.

24/7 PRAYER INITIATIVE

In Europe, another movement has taken on a distinctly different flavor that incorporates prayer with community. "24/7 Prayer" is an international, interdenominational movement of prayer, mission, and justice that began with a single, student-led prayer vigil in Chichester, England in 1999 and has spread, by word of mouth, into 100-plus nations.

For more than a decade the global 24/7 Prayer meeting has continued unbroken, impacting locations as diverse as the US Naval Academy, a German punk festival, war zones and underground churches, the slums of Delhi, the jungles of Papua New Guinea, ancient English cathedrals, and even a brewery in Missouri.

Along the way, this unusual prayer meeting has given rise to numerous new initiatives, communities, and ministries particularly focusing on the poor, the marginalized, students, and those outside the reach of normal expressions of church.

Pete Greig is one of the founding champions of the 24/7 Prayer movement (www.24-7prayer.com), and the Director of Prayer for Holy Trinity, Brompton in London, and a facilitator for the Campus America initiative. Thanks to an innovative approach to spirituality and culture, 24/7 has captured the attention of newspapers and magazines from *Rolling Stone* to *Reader's Digest* and was the subject of a British television documentary.

Part of the core belief underlying their movement is this quote from Dietrich Bonhoeffer, written January 14, 1935: "The restoration of the church will surely come from a sort of new monasticism which has in common with the old only the uncompromising attitude of a life lived according to the Sermon on the Mount."

The prayer movement has moved from intercessory prayer to intercessory action. At the heart of the 24/7 movement there is an expanding network of missional communities inspired by ancient Celtic monasticism and committed to celebrating Christ-centered lifestyles of prayer, mission, and justice. These communities are generically known as "Boiler Rooms" but can have all sorts of local names including "Houses of Prayer." The six core practices of all 24/7 communities are creativity and prayer, hospitality and mercy, learning and mission.

THECALL

Of the more visible movements, Lou Engle's "TheCall" has attracted thousands of believers from around the world to pray together in a stadium event. Their unity causes politicians and policy makers in the region to take note and listen. Lou continues to receive ongoing vision and strategy to mobilize others in prayer to shape how the future unfolds.

Lou Engle is the visionary and co-founder of TheCall solemn assemblies (www.thecall.com) that summoned people to prayer, fasting, repentance, and sacrificial worship in stadiums across the US in the spirit of Joel 2. The strategy derived from Joel 2 involves dropping barriers that divide believers and uniting in urgent, humble fasting and prayer with the promise that God will pour out His spirit.

Lou's passion is to call young adults into a lifestyle of radical prayer, fasting, holiness, and acts of justice. With over 30 years of history in praying for revival, Lou has helped plant two churches, the pro-life ministry Bound4LIFE, and helped raise up the first Justice House of Prayer (JHOP) in Washington DC to pray for the Supreme Court and for righteous leaders in America. Since 2004, JHOPs have emerged in San Francisco, Boston, New York, Montgomery, and San Diego.

THECRY

Faytene Grasseschi (www.faytene.ca), a young Canadian woman, received the vision and the strategy to shape the history of Canada through a youth movement that influenced politics and society. In her book, *Marked: A Generation of Dread Champions Rising to Shift Nations,* she talks about the story of a company of young people who arose and took their place in the nation of Canada and saw it shifted for the glory of God. That shift is happening still as she and her husband Robert mobilize youth to take an active role in intercessory actions that will shape the history of North America.

TheCRY was launched in 2002 by Steve Osmond when 10,000 Canadians responded to the call and gathered to pray for Canada directly in front of the Peace Tower in the nation's capital. It was a historic day of gathering as people from many generations, with a heart for God, came under the banner of Jesus simply to pray for the well-being of the nation.

TheCRY lay dormant for four years until it was resurrected by a passionate group of young adults under the leadership of Faytene Kryskow (now Faytene Grasseschi). Under the new leadership team, thousands gathered again in Ottawa for one reason—to pray. This was to begin a string of nine more CRYs that would take place both in the nation's capital and across the country.

From 2006 to 2011, TheCRY gathered the nation for prayer in Ottawa, Vancouver, Toronto, St. John's, Iqualuit, and Edmonton. In 2012 the vision expanded internationally with TheCRY Hollywood hosting a gathering at Gibson Amphitheatre (Universal City, Hollywood, California) for a passionate day of prayer focused on a sphere that affects many nations; that sphere is entertainment media.

Over the years TheCRY gatherings, in cooperation with the national prayer movement at large, have experienced remarkable answers to prayer including tangible shifts in government on the very days of TheCRYs, drug ring busts, passing of righteous legislation, and more.

It's true. Prayer and fasting changes nations.

THE GLOBAL DAY OF PRAYER

Graham Power, a successful businessman in South Africa, launched a prayer movement called "Transform Africa." It resulted in many African nations gathering in stadiums to pray on a specific date with a specific agenda that unified them all. That prayer movement spread to other counties and became known as "The Global Day of Prayer" (www.globaldayofprayer.com).

The Lord encountered him one night as he lay sleeping. Suddenly, he awoke feeling waves of electricity flowing though him, and the Scripture from Second Chronicles reverberating through him:

> *If my people, who are called by my name, will hum-*
> *ble themselves and pray and seek my face and turn*
> *from their wicked ways, then will I hear from heaven,*
> *and I will forgive their sin and will heal their land*
> (2 Chronicles 7:14).

That encounter with God and subsequent visions made him realize that God was giving him strategy and an invitation to partner with His plans for revival to be unleashed in the earth.

The first thing he realized was that prayer would be rolling out across the globe. And so he started with his local stadium and launched Transform Africa, a day of prayer. Within a few years it had spread throughout the continent, the unity unprecedented among various churches and believers, the impact on the atmosphere breaking up the violence and releasing peace in many regions.

The second thing he saw was that people needed to change the way they did business and politics. So Graham started focusing on training others in ethics and launched "Unashamedly Ethical," asking people to pledge to not take bribes and to work with integrity and accountability (www.unashamedlyethical.com).

Finally, as a result of humbling ourselves in prayer and turning into a more ethical way of living, a positive tsunami of revival would result.

That catalyst encounter enabled him to receive the wisdom and strategy to shape the history of the world—starting with prayer. According to the Global Day of Prayer website:

> In March of 2001, more than 45,000 Christians united for a Day of Repentance and Prayer at Newlands Rugby Stadium in Cape Town. It was a day of intense intercession that transformed lives and was reflected in a changing city in the months to come. Testimonies of transformation caused the vision to be spread into the rest of South Africa and planning immediately started

for similar prayer gatherings in 8 provinces of South Africa for 2002.

In February 2002, Graham Power had a second vision. This vision had an even bigger challenge:

The whole of Africa was to gather in a Day of Repentance and Prayer, changing Africa to become a "light to the world."

Eventually, Africa was to invite all the nations of the globe to unite in this move of transformational prayer.

In May of 2002, Christians in South Africa gathered in 8 different venues for a Day of Repentance and Prayer. Again, the testimonies of church unity and the healing of communities inspired leaders to expand the vision into the rest of Africa. At a summit in September 2002, leaders of 9 African countries agreed on the vision "Africa for Christ."

At the same time, it was clear that different prayer streams from across the globe were flowing in the same direction with a similar vision of community transformation through prayer. God was busy raising up a church of intercession in order to prepare communities for the revelation of His glory.

Across the African continent millions of Christians were inspired to participate in the process of transforming Africa. 77 South African regions and 27 African countries committed to a Day of Repentance and Prayer for Africa on the first of May 2003.

On 2 May 2004, history was made when Christians from all 56 nations of Africa participated in the first ever continental Day of Repentance and Prayer for Africa. Numerous communities, villages, towns, and cities united in non-denominational prayer gatherings at different venues. In South Africa 277 communities participated. A flame of prayer was burning in Africa!

At a meeting of the International Prayer Council in Malaysia in November 2004, the invitation from Africa went out to the nations of the world to participate in a Global Day of Prayer process.

On Pentecost Sunday, 15 May 2005, Christians from 156 of the 220 nations of the world united across denominational and cultural borders for the first Global Day of Prayer. In the months following this day, Christians were overwhelmed by the testimonies of God's powerful work in answer to these prayers and in the years to follow the numbers kept increasing.

In 2008, millions of Christians from 214 nations united in prayer and on 31 May 2009, a miracle happened when this initiative miraculously expanded to 220 countries in the world. Together with the 10 Days leading up to and the 90 Days of Blessing following the Global Day of Prayer, there was a sense that the call to unity and repentance is deepening. This lay the foundation for God to fill the nations with His glory as His children from around the world cried out to Him in unity.

23 May 2010 saw the 10-year celebration of the Global Day of Prayer. Whilst Christians from around the world united in prayer in Cape Town, where everything started, millions from 220 nations once again gathered in their own nations. The urgent call from Joel 2 echoed throughout the nations to return to God with repentance on a level never seen before. Yes, this was a time of rendering our hearts to God and to see the fulfillment of the promise of the Holy Spirit on all flesh.

The growing momentum of the first 10 years laid the foundation to saturate nations in prayer. From 2011 we started to shift our focus from 220 nations to facilitate a lifestyle of prayer with as many people in as many places as possible. In this new season, we no longer aim at the goal of having organized events in every single country of the world, but rather to increase the number of gatherings on Pentecost Sunday in smaller settings, such as local churches, family homes, and businesses instead of stadiums and assembly halls.

12 June 2011 and again on 27 May 2012 saw participation from many nations, cities, towns, communities, local churches, and prayer groups where believers have never had the confidence to register an event, either because they weren't able to gather in large public places because of fear of persecution, or because they don't have the resources to plan such gatherings.

The Lord has indeed done many things through the Global Day of Prayer, and we are certain that these will continue for many, many years to come as nations continue to observe this one day of unified prayer.

ASIA GATHERING AND HOMECOMING

Not specifically a prayer gathering, Gideon Chiu, a Canadian pastor, felt called to bring unity to the Chinese churches in China and in North America. His initial gatherings resulted in tremendous unity among Chinese church leaders with a focus on prayer and waiting on the Lord, rather than a focus on holding a conference based on a singular leader's preaching. As a result, the Asian church leaders around the world have joined in. Where God will take this unity among leaders is yet to be revealed, but the possibilities of the next great revival sweeping through

China and down through the Middle East lies in the heart of the mainland Chinese house church movement.

In May 2010, over 5,000 Chinese believers gathered together to posture themselves for four days before the Lord in worship and prayer. Unlike a traditional conference with a lineup of speakers and preplanned agendas, the only direction given before the gathering was a cry from the heart of the Father calling His Chinese children home. As this remnant obeyed and waited on the Lord together at The Homecoming, the Lord released a sovereign spirit of repentance that broke through traditional barriers between streams and nations and caused the hearts of all those present to be knit together into one true family. Then by faith, this remnant stood and declared together, on behalf of the wider Chinese Body of Christ, "The Chinese are one family! The Chinese have come home! Back home to the Father!"

The next year, the Lord released another call for believers from Asia and around the world to gather in Hong Kong, this time during the Feast of Pentecost, June 8-11, 2011, with a promise given in Jeremiah 32:39: "I will give them one heart and one way" (NKJV). During the gathering, the Lord challenged a remnant from among the Chinese believers to lay aside their own agendas and plans and surrender their lives unconditionally to Him. His desire was that this act of corporate surrender would become a seed through which He might restore the miracle of one accord (divine unity) into the Body of Christ worldwide, preparing the Bride for her end-time mandate and hastening the Lord's return.

In 2012, believers from many nations once again met in Hong Kong for the "Kingdom Come" gathering. Before God's Kingdom can be established in the world, first He must secure His rule and reign over a remnant of His Body. So the Lord stirred the Chinese believers, as a prophetic seed, to declare His supreme rulership as King of kings and Lord of lords over His Bride, from every color and tribe and nation. At the same time, God led believers from more than twenty nations to affirm the leadership role He has called the Chinese to play in His end-time purposes in the earth.

In July 2013, believers from all over the earth once again gathered in Hong Kong for "The Homecoming: Holy Array." Momentum is building for a great move to emerge as unity continues to be established and the prayers of the saints begin to launch the greatest revival the world has ever seen (www.asia gathering.hk).

SHAPING HISTORY BY BECOMING A WALKING GOD-ENCOUNTER FOR OTHERS

Prayer isn't the only catalyst for a move of God that shapes history. God moves sovereignly on whomever He wills; even the unwilling cannot help but respond to His presence. Prophets talk about a coming wave of revival, a youth-led revival, a revival starting among the Hispanics of Los Angeles, then sweeping across the nation, a revival starting everywhere at once around the world. This is an open invitation to respond to God even now.

What if God were to suddenly move in charismatic and evangelical meetings, creating a fusion of God's Spirit and man's that leads us all into a deeper abandonment of ourselves and causes us to explode with supernatural love and power? What if we all became walking spiritual encounters for unbelievers as we released the presence of God and radiated Christ in a dark world? Would you resist this move? Or would you embrace it?

How close do you want to come to the bonfire of God's love and encounter spiritual experiences that you never dreamed of having? It begins with receiving greater revelation of the power of the Word of God. And it moves into dynamic encounters with the Holy Spirit that build our capacity to desire more of Him and lessens our focus on ourselves.

RECEIVING A REVELATION OF THE GLORY OF GOD

Moses met face to face with God who descended in a cloud of glory that enveloped the tent of meeting. And his face radiated the presence and love of God long afterward. Centuries later, Jesus ascended in glory. Today, He is increasingly releasing and imparting that glory, changing us, enlarging our capacities to see and understand more of Him.

> *And we all, who with unveiled faces contemplate the Lord's glory, are being transformed into his image with ever-increasing glory, which comes from the Lord, who is the Spirit* (2 Corinthians 3:18).

How much glory can you presently handle?

Not only are we cleansed and purified in glory, but we are being changed into His likeness (see Isa. 6:5). We are meant to transform "from glory to glory." We are meant to change as we look Him straight in the face and worship the King of Glory. Slowly, through the years, we come into His presence and discover our old nature giving way as we become the persons we were created to become. Yet sometimes, God accelerates the process and descends in a cloud of glory that causes us to radiate the presence and love of God long afterward. Those sudden encounters enlarge our hearts with love and we discover that our role in life is to walk in that love and give it away.

Like Moses, we must encounter God's glory first in order to become carriers of His glory. The greatest, most pure revelatory encounters and spiritual experiences occur when you find yourself in an atmosphere infused with God's glory. We need to seek His face, pray for a release of God's glory, and embrace it when it comes. Then, as we bask in His glory, Christ in us, the hope of glory, can overflow through us to the world.

BECOMING A SPIRITUAL EXPERIENCE TO RELEASE THE BRILLIANCE OF HIS PRESENCE

In Christ and in His Word, there is no shadow of turning, no shifting shadows of light and darkness coexist. In Him is light. He is the light of the world. And we are the light of the world. We are meant to become a walking spiritual experience and the world encounters God in us, the hope of glory. Having stood in the tent of meeting saturated in glory, our faces radiate with His love and heaven touches earth through us. We then become gatekeepers of His presence, recognizing the flow of God's life through us and understanding how to release His presence into a given situation.

In other words, God is in us now and He is coming with ever-increasing measures of glory that will so saturate us that it will seem like the presence of God and man are fused together. Learning to release the Holy Spirit to others will come easily as the anointing of His presence flows from us.

Your role as a believer filled with God's Spirit is to move with Him—in intercessory prayer and in intercessory action—wherever you live and work.

It is possible to experience this now. Several years ago, I entered into a greater understanding of what it means to be a walking revival for others. The understanding of how to move in God's presence and power is more caught than taught and accelerated by soaking in an atmosphere of His presence.

Praying for people in church and seeing the presence and power of God move on their behalf is normal for me in my Christian milieu. But under unusual circumstances in my secular consulting work, I discovered much to my chagrin that I was accidentally releasing the presence of God in the workplace and it wouldn't shut off. The spiritual dynamics that followed me as I worked on several overseas contracts startled me. My job skills had opened doors to minister in the places where God called—not in the cocoon of the church or the nest of my home, but into the midst of very dark places in Europe and Asia. And yes, the people I talked with were saved, healed, delivered, and touched by God's tangible presence and His overwhelming love. Most of the time they didn't know I am a Christian, until they started shaking and crying and asked me what was up with the strange sensations they felt in my "office." I saw some amazing things as God walked with me and moved through me and as I released His prophetic words and power to others, or others simply found that they had walked into a "power zone of God's presence" and reacted to the presence of God within me.

While working overseas, I became extremely aware that what I carried within me instantly and undeniably shifted the environment around me. While I had experienced this on rare occasions in the past, now, His presence would not and could not be turned off whenever I ventured off to work. As a result, I often found myself in uncomfortable positions that could have resulted in my immediate dismissal. But God covers what He initiates. His love for others is so great that He will move heaven and earth, brush aside the "giants in the land," and break all the protocols of man to touch the hearts of those to whom He is reaching out that day.

Once I caught on to what was happening when others came into my/His presence, I realized that I could intentionally release His presence to whomever I desired and learned to harness His power more effectively. However, it wasn't until I attended a Fusion Conference held in Albany, Oregon (August 2006) that I fully understood what was happening to me and through me.

Lance Wallnau's prophetic insights given during that conference helped lessen my fear, clarify my understanding, and learn how to direct the flow of His presence more effectively. Here are the key points I picked up from Lance. Let them serve as prophetic words of wisdom as we glimpse what is to come:

- God is sending us on missions and assignments where we don't want to go. He calls us to release heaven there. Professionals can do this even on a bad day. We have the authority to bring into the present what we see in the future. The greater weight of glory on earth today is pulling heaven to earth.

- Get to the place where you are not shaken (by what you see and hear around you).
- What you are carrying shifts the environment around you. The lesser authority yields to the greater authority. The person with the dominant process can take over the frequency of the room or the group. The depressed or angry one will impact the group. Or you can bring them under the authority of the anointing in your life.
- We have a kingdom "radius of heaven." It is as close as your hand. Atmospheres are things you shape. Not respond to.
- We are carrying the capacity to release the supernatural. We have the kingdom within—a force of righteousness, peace, joy, love, power, and authority.

We are carrying the capacity to release the supernatural. When a Spirit-filled believer walks through the door, the atmosphere shifts! We have the kingdom within—the force of righteousness, peace, joy, love, power, and authority—and it will accidentally flow from us at the oddest times and displace the internal and external forces that trap unbelievers in a cycle of despair.

The presence of God in me and the radius of heaven surrounding me were strengthened by the time I spent at home and at church, soaking in God's powerful presence. All of that year, I came home to recharge and a few weeks later left again for Europe or Asia and released His presence to a dark and hungry world. God and I fused together as I soaked in His glory like a sponge and wrung it out on anyone nearby. Christ in me grew stronger and released the hope of glory to others with or without my conscious consent.

GLIMPSES OF WHAT'S TO COME

Those who cultivate a humble abandonment to the Lord and purpose to give Him all glory will soon discover that they have become this century's new mystics, back door prophets, and power brokers who overflow with the healing gifts and miracles of the Holy Spirit—at work, at home, on the street, and even in church. Already, we are seeing glimpses of what is to come as more people are stirred to faith and action and more places are becoming churches and communities known as places where God's presence dwells.

Open visions and dreams that God has given me over the years lead me to believe that yes, a great move of God is coming, but it begins with you and me, right now. Those who shine with the glory of God become walking spiritual experiences for others.

Arise, dear reader, and shine. For your light, the glory of God will rise upon you. You, personally, have a sacred destiny and calling. How far into it do you want to go?

Have you awakened to Him? Does your heart burn when you feel His presence? Have you stood with your face to the wind of worship and caught a glimpse of the realities of heaven surrounding you? There is more anointing to come. The oil is being released.

We all, corporately, have a sacred destiny and calling as well. Each generation is called to move into greater maturity in Christ, becoming established in Him and releasing the revelation of Jesus. They release not only the stories of the great miracles of God in their generation and past moves documented in history, but a very present anointing that reveals more about who Jesus really is—His character and personality—and the power that He manifests currently, here on earth.

As each generation awakens to the Anointed One, we experience His love and presence and power and we want more. We want to become established in Him. As we are established, we see ourselves becoming transformed more into His image and less into the image this fallen world would impose upon us. Our heart longs to experience more of His love filling us when we awaken to Him. Then we move into deeper relationship that establishes us in His love, and we desire now to give it away, to impart it to others. What does imparting His love look like? Reaching out with compassion, we move in power to heal others emotionally, spiritually, physically. Moving out in power, we stop for the one God stops for, listening for the divine appointment that occurs as we take notice of another and the Holy Spirit drops a word of knowledge or wisdom or discernment into our spirit and we stop to impart that to the other, unlocking his or her heart and awakening it to the Anointed One.

As we learn to move in harmony with His spirit, we find ourselves flowing into greater release. The gifts of the spirit become integrated into our personality and lifestyle. Some carry this anointing of His presence into their everyday work world and shift the atmosphere, releasing light in the darkness. Others release the anointing into governmental spheres of influence, transforming policies and procedures in their companies and organizations that shift them out of the worldly system and into godly, spiritual principles that work.

Part of my destiny and all of our destinies is to release the anointing in everyday life—to our families, our colleagues, our bosses, our employees, to whatever chain of command or governmental structure we labor under. We are called to be like Christ and release His presence wherever we go. The rest of our destiny unfolds gradually or suddenly as a dream or vision imparts a revelation of destiny.

Apart from a dramatic God-encounter releasing a word of destiny, coming into the awareness of your personal destiny seems to progress something like this: As you recognize who you are in Christ and who He is to you, you become established in Him. Your gifts, natural and spiritual, begin to converge and merge with your identity as a beloved son or daughter of the Creator of the Universe. The favor of the Lord blows in, breathing new life in you, quickening your faith and anointing, and ushers you into specific assignments or mandates.

As you begin to fulfill those assignments, suddenly you realize that you are walking into your sacred destiny. Adventure and excitement renew your energy level. Suddenly, you are not old, but moving in the power of the Holy Spirit. Suddenly, you are not young and immature, but moving in a wisdom and power beyond your training and years. Destiny unfolds and you begin to discover that every experience you have lived, every talent you possess converges into a season of time and you find yourself empowered like never before to walk in your sacred destiny. You know who you are and where you are going. You know the purpose of the anointing in your life. You are walking in the Anointing and it feels good.

All of us have the authority to impart the Anointing, who is Christ, and release the gifts of the Spirit according to the person's need who stands before us. Not many of us have the opportunity to consistently stand before a crowd and move in the anointing under the empowerment of the Holy Spirit. Those who do realize that at some point they had to stop moving in their own agendas and learn how to flow with the Holy Spirit to accomplish His desire. They had to learn how to recognize the wave of His Spirit, paddle out and catch it, then ride it in. There are longboard surfers, like me, who like to ride the smaller waves that break for a long ride sideways toward the shore. And then there are big wave surfers who are towed out behind jet-skis into the towering giants and catch waves of enormous power, waves that could crush them if they fall.

Most of my peers who were once on fire and serving the Lord in various positions of ministry, have left all ministry involvement and settled into the easy chairs of middle age or focused on their own recreational pursuits. They will peek in on the waves of renewal or outpouring once in a while, but really want nothing to do with this current move of God. They have been there and done that. Sadly, many pastors, prophets, apostles, evangelists, and teachers who used to watch for the waves and ride them with ease have also stopped paddling out to meet the waves. As a former surfer, I can tell you this timeless truth—the waves never stop coming. Big waves come in sets. Every season stirs up the waters and beckons surfers to enter in. Stormy seas generate the most awesome big waves. There are waves still calling us. It's time for some to get off the beach, break out the board, and paddle out. But sometimes we do need to recognize that transition God calls us into—out of the lineup and into instructor/mentor mode.

We carry different anointings and authority during different seasons of our own lives. Big wave surfers eventually must turn the lineup over to younger surfers—for a reason. The spirit is willing, but age and wisdom take over and wisely invite them to step into another manifestation of the anointing they are able to carry and sustain in that season of life. And we are seeing that transition coming quickly in the Church today. The big waves are coming. And many in leadership today are quickly mobilizing to train the next generation to catch the incoming sets.

If you have awakened to His love and power, you have a destiny that can only be fulfilled by you. You have a place and position in the corporate, mystical Body of Christ on earth and a sacred calling. Time is short. I suggest you get on with discovering who you really are and who you are destined to become. God is not finished with you yet. All of your gifts, experiences, and anointings have converged at this stage of your life for a purpose. God is calling you to become someone more than you ever dreamed. He has need of you to step into the authority and anointing He has destined for you to release at this stage of your life. Will you come into the next level of your anointing?

It all starts with prayer and ends with discovering that your role in life is to walk closely aligned with Holy Spirit. And the world is transformed wherever you go with God.

CHAPTER 13

THE AMERICA OF TOMORROW: HOW SHALL WE PRAY?

by C. Peter Wagner

We now live in the midst of the greatest prayer movement in recorded history, both nationally and internationally. By saying this, I am in no way intending to trivialize the legendary prayer movements of the past, but the reality is that they did not enjoy the incredible means of communication that we now have with the Internet and other vehicles of digital technology. The multiplied facets of the modern prayer movement are now so widespread and rapidly developing that it is all but impossible to catalog them.

SIGNIFICANT PRAYER INITIATIVES

My knowledge is obviously limited. Still, at the risk of leaving out some significant prayer initiatives that should be mentioned, I will list some that come to mind. Doris and I had the privilege of leading the AD2000 United Prayer Track during the 1990s which convened several notable international prayer gatherings and facilitated on-site prayer journeys to each of the 50-some nations of the 10/40 Window. This culminated in the October 1999 Celebration Ephesus event which brought together over 5,000 individuals from 61 nations in the amphitheater in ancient Ephesus where the silversmiths rioted against the apostle Paul. The focus then shifted to the 40/70 Window with more international prayer gatherings and prayer journeys as well. Graham Power of South Africa soon launched the massive Transformation Africa prayer movement and the Global Day of Prayer on the Day of Pentecost which for several years found almost every nation in the world joining together for intercession. Momentum built until arguably the largest intercessory prayer gathering ever took place in a stadium in Jakarta, Indonesia on May 17, 2012 with some 100,000 participating.

Narrowing our focus to the US, I could safely say that we are surrounded by more committed, proactive, prophetic intercessors per capita than ever before in our history. Authentic prayer ministries continue to mushroom from state to state. One of the highest-visibility intercessory initiatives has been TheCall, led by Lou Engle. Robert Stearns, Jack Hayford, and Paul Cedar have catalyzed an enormous international agreement in prayer for the "Peace of Jerusalem" the first Sunday of every October. Among the agencies that God has raised up to help coordinate this massive prayer effort are the Reformation Prayer Network led by Cindy Jacobs and the Heartland Apostolic Prayer Network led by John Benefiel. Each of them has coordinators in all 50 states, and they work closely together. The intercessors are using the prayer tools and methodologies which first emerged in the 1990s, combining them with ongoing revelation and experience on the front lines, all of which has greatly matured today's intercessory army.

DISCERNING THE DIRECTION

I want to direct this essay toward the leaders of this unprecedented prayer force in America. To be personal and transparent, let me admit that I am no longer an active leader or even a bona fide player in these modern prayer initiatives. However, I did provide apostolic leadership in this field during the 1990s, and that has left me with a certain residue of respect. I now, at 82, find myself in a very enviable position in life. In 2010, I turned over eight ministries which I had been leading to my spiritual sons and daughters, and now I am in what I call my "fourth career." I am aligned with apostle Chuck Pierce in Global Spheres, Inc., and I am enjoying what Bobby Clinton terms "Phase VI" of leadership development, "afterglow." This means that I can sit back, keep my finger on the pulse of what the Spirit seems to be saying to the churches, and speak out when I feel I discern the direction that God wants us to take, moving into the future.

That is what I am attempting to do here. Look at the title of this essay: "The America of Tomorrow: How Shall We Pray?" I anticipate that the title will present a dilemma to many readers. The knee-jerk response to my question would be that we naturally want to pray for the America of tomorrow; however, on further thought it will occur to many that our prayer movements up to now have frequently been concentrating on the "America of Yesterday."

THE PROPHETIC MANDATE

I had been thinking about this for a time when I received a strong prophetic mandate from Chuck Pierce during the 2012 annual Global Spheres/Glory of Zion Passover Gathering. Chuck is the prophet with whom I am most closely aligned, so I pay special attention when the word of the Lord comes through him to me. I think it is important that I record most of this prophetic interchange.

Paul Keith Davis had just finished his message on April 6, 2012, and he began to prophesy. Among other things, he said, "And, Lord, I just release over this house that apostolic anointing, that model that we saw in Antioch, the one that gave us an interpretation of scriptures that transformed cities. May it be deposited here!"

At which point, Chuck Pierce stood up and said, "Now, Peter, I want you to hear that word because of what Anne Tate and I heard earlier this morning. The Lord said, 'The Antioch door is now reopening over you.' I have waited for that to be said. We heard it twice already today, and this is the third time. 'The Antioch door is being reopened in this place.' I have no idea what it means, but this is the third time it has come forth today."

Chuck then faced me and continued:

Peter, I feel like I have to give you an assignment. I say this humbly to you, but I know you're quite capable of doing this for us. There was a word over you, and the Lord said to you, "Open your eyes, for I will now reveal to you how the past has come to its closure and the new will begin to be expressed." While you're here, you are going to get a message.

I know you are capable because you're a historian and you've got the best commentary on Acts that has ever been written because it makes Acts real today. You are going to know what is really opening over us here. You're going to understand how one church era is ending and a new church era is being established. You're going to break us out of our nationalism. You're going to cause us to see a kingdom expression in the days ahead that we have not seen. This is the last major assignment that the Lord is giving you and you're going to reinitiate the open door that came into an expression in Antioch, but has never come into fullness for this church age.

And then: "Lord, I loose this assignment. I feel like angelically You are giving it from heaven to be imparted to him. I know that he might be aged in years, but he is fresh in revelation. We decree right now that the last great message and paradigm shift for this generation's alignment will now be released into Peter in Jesus's name."

I have been allowing this prophetic assignment to permeate my spirit, and I have been praying over it for several months. I now feel that I have enough of a grasp on what the Spirit is saying to the churches in order to begin conversation on the matter.

UNDERSTANDING ANTIOCH

First we need to start with the biblical Antioch, the capital of Syria, and the events which unfolded in that city. Let me say up front that I am making a long story short. If you doubt any of the statements I make here, please go my commentary on Acts that Chuck mentioned to get a full explanation.[1]

Antioch, with a population of 500,000, was the third largest city of the Roman Empire. It hosted a colony of 25,000 Jews (5 percent of the population) who lived in segregated housing in the Jewish Quarter. Their contact with the 475,000 Gentiles was minimal at best.

The first missionaries to Antioch were Jewish believers who were driven out of Jerusalem. Acts says, "Now those who were scattered after the persecution that arose over Stephen traveled as far as Phoenicia, Cyprus, and Antioch, preaching the word to no one but the Jews only" (Acts 11:19 NKJV). That means that when they arrived in Antioch, they settled in the Jewish Quarter and planted house churches among those who lived there. They would not have shared the gospel with the Antioch Gentiles. This continued for ten years.

Ten years later, a second missionary team arrived in Antioch, assigned by God to preach, not to the minority Jews, but to the majority Gentiles. Acts tells us that "...men from Cyprus and Cyrene, who, when they had come to Antioch, spoke to the Hellenists [the Gentiles], preaching the Lord Jesus. And the hand of the Lord was with them, and a great number believed and turned to the Lord" (Acts 11:20-21 NKJV). These missionaries multiplied

Gentile house churches. Although it might offend our current political correctness, the fact remains that there was very little interaction between these new Gentile house churches and the older ones in the Jewish quarter. Keep in mind that we are dealing with the first century, not the 21st century.

Whatever the social situation, these new Gentile believers in Antioch were part of the Body of Christ, just as much as the Jewish converts were. The problem? The Gentile men were not circumcised and they did not keep the Jewish law. The word of this complicating turn of events got out to the church in Jerusalem, which, of course, was all Jewish. Acts says, "Then news of these things came to the ears of the church in Jerusalem, and they sent out Barnabas to go as far as Antioch" (Acts 11:22 NKJV).

This was the new paradigm, and Barnabas turned out to be favorable to what was happening: "When he came and had seen the grace of God, he was glad, and encouraged them all that with purpose of heart they should continue with the Lord" (Acts 11:23 NKJV). Gentiles, according to Barnabas, could be believers without being circumcised! "The disciples were first called Christians in Antioch" (Acts 11:26 NKJV)!

This, however, was not the end. Barnabas brought Saul (later Paul) from Tarsus to Antioch. They eventually added "Simeon who was called Niger, Lucius of Cyrene, Manaen who had been brought up with Herod the tetrarch" to their team (Acts 13:1 NKJV). It is important to observe that none of these five were from Antioch. They were foreign missionaries, and because they came from the outside they could build bridges between the Jewish house churches and the Gentile house churches, which they did. Saul, who was a Jew, even took a bold step and started eating with Gentile believers to symbolize that Jew and Gentile were "one new man." We can assume that others did as well. This caused great controversy, as is the case with most paradigm shifts. Later Paul even got into a fight with Peter and Barnabas, calling them "hypocrites" because once they ate with Gentiles, then they quit. You can read all about it in Galatians 2:11-14.

The contention about Gentiles not being circumcised continued to escalate for three or four years until the Council of Jerusalem, which was held in AD 49, decreed that Gentiles could remain as they were and still be legitimate believers (see Acts 15:19). But the paradigm shift began in Antioch.

In Chuck Pierce's prophecy to me, he started with "the Antioch door," and then said, "You are going to understand how one church era is ending and a new church era is being established." In Antioch the old church era admitted circumcised Jews only, but the new church era embraced both Jews and Gentiles, forming what Paul later called "one new man" (see Eph. 2:15 NKJV).

How does this apply to what the Spirit is saying to the churches today? As I have prayed about this assignment, two paradigm shifts continue coming to mind. One involves our nation and the other involves the church.

THE AMERICA OF TOMORROW

The America of tomorrow will not be the same as the America we have known. The 20th century, during which many of us received our personal formation, will undoubtedly go down in history as America's century. America dominated the world in military might, scientific breakthroughs, educational attainments, missionary outreach, international economics, agricultural production, medical advancements, manufacturing, personal and familial prosperity, and many other indicators of national superiority. Christianity flourished. It was an enviable position for most of us Americans.

Even those from other countries looked up to America enough to make it the destination of choice for those who were emigrating from their home nations.

I have just described the "America of Yesterday." I know that will be a disheartening statement to many, and I regret having to say it myself. I earlier chronicled the massive and exciting prayer movement of our times, which is very good. However, as I attempt to track the objects of our prayers I have observed that a good many of our petitions and proclamations have been directed toward reestablishing the America of yesterday. Even many of our prayers for revival and awakening look nostalgically toward the past. We ask God to raise up a Wesley or a Whitfield, to bring us a Cane Ridge Revival, to bring forth another David Brainerd or Jonathan Edwards, to give us a vision for Jeremiah Lanphier and the Fulton Street Prayer meeting, to restore the Jesus People, to repeat Toronto or Brownsville, to allow us to taste a Welsh Revival, to reinstate Azusa Street, to pour out a Third Great Awakening, and on and on. I like to say that it's OK to learn from the past, but not to yearn for the past. Am I the only one who perceives a great deal of yearning these days?

I believe we should begin looking toward and praying into the America of tomorrow. Make no mistake about it—I am a patriotic American. I thank God for those like David Barton who remind us, with exquisitely minute historical data, that the roots of our nation are clearly Christian. My four-times great-grandfather was Alexander Hamilton, a born-again Christian who was the closest confidant of George Washington and some historians say the father of our American government. I am a conservative both theologically and politically. I am a registered Republican. I want America to blossom and become everything that God wants it to be. I want God's kingdom to come and His will to be done here in America as it is in heaven. Numerous bloggers on the Internet will take a statement like that and accuse me of being a "dominionist." My response? Guilty, as charged!

THE ELECTION OF 2012

I wrote the above paragraphs weeks before the American election of 2012 in which Barack Obama was reelected President for the next four years. This election provided us with the strongest statement on record so far that the America of yesterday is a thing of the past. I believe it would be good for us to agree that

God is not looking for yesterday's America, but rather for tomorrow's America. We have wonderful memories of the 18th, the 19th, and the 20th centuries of America's history. But none of them provides a template for the America of the 21st century. Let's not look back; let's look ahead. This is part of the paradigm shift taking us from an old era to a new era.

What else did the election show us about the America of tomorrow? It showed us that there will be no turning back. America's demographics and American culture, for better or for worse, have changed forever. Obama received overwhelming support from African-Americans, Latinos, Asians, and the millennial generation. On the day after the election, conservative commentator Bill O'Reilly exclaimed, "We're in a different country!" This means we are another Antioch. We're dealing with a distinct culture. This time, instead of seeking God's ways of taking the gospel from the Jews to the Gentiles, we need to find God's plan for taking the gospel of the Kingdom from the America of yesterday to the America of tomorrow.

I continue to address our prayer leaders. The day after the election, prophet Chuck Pierce wrote, "I see a new prophetic intercessory movement ahead to help us make the shift into Kingdom alignment." Notice the word "new." He adds, "There is no need to pray for the America we have known, but we must pray and intercede to develop a New Wineskin America." And then, "The new battlefields will not be the present battlefields." He suggests that our prayer movements will need to address things like the IRS, the Electoral College, the health care structure, and the Federal Reserve System.[2] Are the leaders of our prayer movements prepared to launch out and pray into these areas and others which God will show us?

I hope I do not hear that the reason American culture is changing, even embracing certain unbiblical values, might be because "we didn't pray enough." Please review the first two pages, where I describe some of the unprecedented prayer movements in our nation and abroad, and believe me when I say that the intensity of prayer for America before the election of 2012 was truly amazing. I personally think that we did pray enough, and more besides. However, I do suspect that we, as a nation, might not adequately have humbled ourselves. Let's remember 2 Chronicles 7:14: "If My people who are called by My name will humble themselves, and pray...[I will] heal their land" (NKJV).

The first step is to humble ourselves, but keep in mind that I said "as a nation." We have individually knelt in humility, washed feet, done identificational repentance, confessed our personal and corporate sins. But, like it or not, America is still not seen by much of the rest of the world as a humble nation. Keep in mind that humility does not imply weakness. Humility is "power under control" just as Jesus exemplified. America is certainly a powerful nation, but our power has not always been accompanied by a humble spirit.

This was brought home by my friend, Wolfgang Simson of Germany, who wrote an essay the day after the election, "Our dear America—where do you go from here?" He begins with a picture of the cover of Der Spiegel (similar to America's Time magazine) where Uncle Sam is in a hospital bed with an IV drip and the caption: "The American Patient: The Decline of a Great Nation." Where does humility come in? Here is a question that Simson raises: "Did you ever allow the thought that God in His sovereignty is using Obama like a pawn on His chessboard to humble the US as a nation because He wants to show His grace to a nation gone completely self-sufficient? A nation that is so full of independence, individualism, nationalism, and trusting a greed- and fear-based economy that there may be only one way open to heal it from its idolatry and re-align itself with the Kingdom of God: a crisis beyond anything that America has ever seen!" I know that you and I don't like to hear things like this. But in his original prophecy to me regarding doing this paper, Chuck Pierce said, "You're going to break us out of our nationalism." I think that Wolfgang Simson gives us a clue to the solution when he says, "The problem of the current commotion and insecurity arises when even God's people keep confusing the Kingdom of God with the United States of America."[3]

If this is the case, let's look forward to taking a different course.

NO LONGER NUMBER ONE!

What might this course be? It might even be beyond our control. Let's focus on the bigger picture. One way that we may humble ourselves as a nation is to get used to the rather disturbing fact that the America of tomorrow will no longer be the number one superpower of the world. If not, which nation will? The answer is China. This transition will not happen overnight. At the moment China does not have the mindset to rule the world. But China has a significant advantage in not needing to deal with a record of imperialism. I am simply reporting what I see to be the hand of God moving the nations of the world toward His kingdom.

For a long time I have been teaching about the historical shifts of the center of gravity of world Christianity. The first center of gravity was Jerusalem, then it moved to Ephesus, then to Rome and Constantinople, then to Western Europe, then to North America, and now it has moved to the Asian-Pacific rim with China as the chief player in that region. In that area of the world we have been seeing the most explosive numerical growth of Christianity ever recorded. The church is taking new forms that will in all probability provide the template for the churches of tomorrow. Missionary outreach is becoming the strongest in the world, including the visionary Back to Jerusalem Movement. Finances for Christian causes are already reaching new levels. I began to learn this in the late 1990s when I was overseeing the building of the World Prayer Center in Colorado Springs.

Some 70 percent of the funds that I raised came from Asia!

THE CHINA PROPHECY

I recently wrote a report of a mission trip I took to China, and I am going to excerpt some thoughts from it. It relates to a remarkable prophecy from Chuck Pierce that he recorded in his book *God's Unfolding Battle Plan*.[4] This is a word concerning China that he received in 1986, back when China was far from a respected member of the international community. Here is the prophecy, along with some comments:

> 1986. The Chinese government would begin to change from its oppressive policies. [This year the student revolutions began that led to the Tiananmen Square event.]

> 1996. The government of the church will begin to shift toward an apostolic model. [Reportedly, the beginnings of the greatest "leadershift" in the Chinese church can be traced back to 1996.]

> 2006. China will come into the world picture. [This is the year when preparations began for the 2008 Beijing Olympic Games which put China on virtually every television screen in the world.]

> 2016. The economy of China will be second to none, and the US will become an ally of China. [This is the next date for us today, and I will comment on it later.]

> 2026. The Chinese people will be the most dominant and influential people on earth, and China will have the principal role of bringing in world harvest (p. 212). [For more than ten years, by the way, I have been prophesying that by 2025 China would be sending more foreign missionaries than any other nation.]

The prophecies for 2016 and 2026 clearly imply that in the 21st century, China will become number one. Some of us have been basking in what has been called "American exceptionalism," and it has been a well-deserved label for the America of yesterday. But I could imagine that some of my Chinese friends might be considering "Chinese exceptionalism" as a slogan for tomorrow, and it would be hard to deny. Please don't misunderstand me. I'm an American, and I like to be number one. In the 2012 Olympics we still earned more medals than the Chinese, but not by as much as in the past. Please catch these words: In this essay I am trying to deal with the *is*, not the *ought!*

Back to 2016. When Chuck Pierce prophesied in 1986 that thirty years later, in 2016, China's economy would be second to none, most informed observers tended to ignore it at best and ridicule it at worst. However, let me quote from a piece by Brett Arends from MarketWatch of the Wall Street Journal dated April 25, 2011:

> IMF bombshell: Age of America nears end

> Commentary: China's economy will surpass the US in 2016.

> The International Monetary Fund has just dropped a bombshell, and nobody noticed. For the first time, the international organization has set a date for the moment when the "Age of America" will end and the US economy will be overtaken by that of China. And it's a lot closer than you may think.

> According to the latest IMF official forecasts, China's economy will surpass that of America in real terms in 2016—just five years from now.

I had a chance to discuss this with an outstanding kingdom-minded Chinese economist, and he told me that his data points to the date 2020, not 2016, when China's economy will be number one. But he also suggested that Chinese thinking (as contrasted to Western thinking) would regard 2020 as close enough to validate the prophecy. We shall see. But no matter what the date might be, America needs to humble itself and be a good number two.

A SURPRISE?

Yes, this is a stunning surprise to many Americans, including some American prayer leaders. But let me point out that it is not a surprise to God. Otherwise, why would God reveal this to us through His prophet many years ago? I believe He revealed it in 1986 because He wanted His people prepared for this historic change. The Bible says that if we believe His prophets we will prosper (see 2 Chron. 20:20). The knee-jerk reaction of some will be to cry out to energize the intercessors to a new level so that this does not happen and that America remains as number one. They yearn for the America of yesterday! I don't think that is realistic. Instead, let's believe the prophets and pray that God will allow America to develop into a number two that advances the Kingdom of God in every way. More recently, Chuck Pierce gave this further word from the Lord: "The Dragon and her children, other Asian nations, will arise to unprecedented control of the economic systems of the earth...China is creating a society to advance the kingdom of God. The house church system there is the strongest in the world. Their call to Israel is amazing."[5]

Due, at least in part, to the attempted eradication of Christianity under Mao Zedong and the subsequent ruthless persecution of house church Christians, many Western believers have a bitter taste in their mouth when they think of China. This is understandable, but things have changed. Just as we attempt to view America realistically, we must learn not to focus on the China of yesterday but the China of tomorrow. For the record, the greatest national harvest of souls ever recorded in history has taken place in China over the past 30 years. All three major branches of the Chinese church are flourishing—the government-sanctioned Three Self Church, the traditional rural house church movement, and the new "third church" or urban house church movement. It may well be that the form and function of the churches of the urban house church movement will furnish the most important new template for the worldwide church of the 21st century. Among Kingdom-minded believers, we have a consensus that the ultimate measurement of successful societal transformation would be the elimination of systemic poverty. The Chinese government has succeeded in lifting over 300 million individuals (roughly the population of the US) out of systemic poverty through their urbanization program.

For some, especially those with memories of the Cold War, a major stumbling block to acknowledging the fact that China is destined to become number one is that it is not a democracy, but has a one-party government, namely the Communist Party. The fact that under this Communist government China has blossomed into one of the world's most capitalistic societies, even owning a great deal of our current American debt, must not escape attention. Some things that seem contradictory to us may not seem contradictory to the mindset of other cultures. And the good news is that recently some Kingdom-minded Chinese believers who have felt called to help transform the Chinese government mountain have chosen to join the Communist party. Reports I am receiving indicate that their faith is known to their colleagues and is respected. One of my friends in the party projects a "30-30 Vision," namely that by 2030, China will be 30 percent Christian. He foresees that the China of tomorrow will experience "transformation with the Cross!"

It might be a good thing if some of our American prayer movements would join with our Chinese brothers and sisters in asking God to bring about this kind of transformation and that God would begin to show us what role the America of tomorrow will have in this new chapter of world history.

Let's keep in mind Chuck Pierce's prophecy about 2016 where he says that once China achieves the top world economy, "The United States will realign itself with China and they will be allies."[6]

Some of my Chinese friends have begun calling this a new "G2." If so, let's pray that through this G2 God's Kingdom will come on earth as it is in heaven!

THE CHURCH

You will recall that Chuck Pierce prophesied about "the Antioch door," pointing out that in Antioch one church era ended and another began. He then assigned me to make an application of that principle to our present situation. When he did, I mentioned that two paradigm shifts came into my mind. The first had to do with the nation, and I have just set forth the big picture of how I see the America of tomorrow, especially in relationship to China. If the nation of America was involved in the first paradigm shift, the church is the subject of the second one.

The paradigm for the church of the future may well be found in what many are calling the "New Apostolic Reformation" (NAR). This paradigm shift has already begun. Consider these words carefully: We are now experiencing the most radical change in the way of doing church since the Protestant Reformation. Notice the words, "doing church." We are not talking about a change in the theology of the Reformation. We believe in the authority of Scripture, justification by faith, and the priesthood of all believers as strongly as did Luther or Calvin. However, we are talking about the ways in which the church is beginning to live out these theological convictions day after day.

This is not the place to attempt to catalog all the differences between what we might think of as the old wineskin of the church and the new wineskin. Some of them, however, are more important than others, and I will try to highlight them. I think I am correct in contending that the most important distinction between the old and the new is the governance of the church. In the new wineskin, apostles, in the New Testament sense of the word, head up the government of the church.

AUTHORITY

In fact, of all the radical changes characteristic of the New Apostolic Reformation, I consider this the most radical of all: The amount of spiritual authority delegated by the Holy Spirit to individuals. Notice that the operative words in this statement are "authority" and "individuals." We Protestants are not accustomed to individuals having much spiritual authority. Traditionally, the final authority in our church bodies has resided in groups, not individuals. That is where we get such ecclesiastical terminology as "deacon boards" or "synods" or "sessions" or "congregations" or "general councils" or "presbyteries" or "vestries" or "state conventions" or "monthly meetings" or any number of similar terms—all referring to groups over individuals. The inevitable implication? Individuals cannot be trusted with final authority in the churches.

Churches of the NAR do not follow that traditional line of reasoning. They take seriously Scriptures such as Ephesians 2:20 which tells us that the household of God (the church) is "built on the foundation of the apostles and prophets, Jesus Christ Himself being the chief cornerstone" (NKJV). And also, "And God has appointed these in the church: first apostles, second prophets, third teachers..." (1 Cor. 12:28 NKJV). Apostles, properly related to prophets, are those who are intended to govern the church and to have the final authority. While all NAR churches recognize the function of the apostolic leader, some of them, for various reasons, have chosen not to adopt the title "apostle" as yet. I mention this only to help some from being sidetracked from recognizing apostolic governance because other leadership titles might be used. As an example, some of the most powerful apostolic leaders of our generation have been leaders of the Chinese rural house church movement. It has been reported that these individuals have had up to tens of millions of believers aligned under them. Their preferred title? "Uncle!"

The New Apostolic Reformation began with the African Independent Church Movement around 1900. It continued through the Chinese house church movement, the Latin American grassroots church movement, and the US independent charismatic movement, to name only some of its most visible components. This is not insignificant. These new wineskin churches, the NAR, represent the largest megablock of non-Catholic Christianity in the world, and the only megablock of Christianity growing faster than the world population and Islam.[7]

This will allow us to see, simply in terms of ecclesiastical demographics, why it is reasonable to consider the New Apostolic Reformation as a possible template for the new church age in worldwide Christianity.

AFFILIATION AND ACCOUNTABILITY

I will conclude this essay by mentioning two important characteristics of NAR churches other than governance. The first has to do with church affiliation. In the old wineskin the most common vehicle for affiliation among churches was denominations. Denominations served the Body of Christ very well for hundreds of years, and some still do. However, most denominations have been in a pattern of decline over the past 20 years, and significant turnaround seems unlikely. The new vehicle for affiliation is apostolic networks, led not by some person or group of persons elected through a democratic process, but rather by a mutual recognition of the gift and office of apostle on the part of the affiliated churches. The apostle, properly related to prophets, is the final authority for the life and ministry of the network.

Denominations typically are structured around a constitution and bylaws, and they operate through legal structures. Some denominations as a whole and/or judicatories under the denomination are also territorial. They can function only within certain geographical boundaries. On the other hand, apostolic networks strive to avoid both legalism and territorialism. The glue that holds them together is relational. Affiliation with an apostolic network is voluntary and is conditional upon the relationship of the church's pastor with the apostle. The pattern is for apostolic networks to be very stable because pastors are typically grateful for the value that the apostle adds to their lives and ministries.

The final characteristic of NAR churches that I want to mention is alignment and accountability. If the apostle is the recognized leader of the apostolic network, obviously the pastors are aligned with the apostle and are accountable to him or her. But what about the apostle? Where is the accountability?

The accountability is established when the apostle, by mutual consent, aligns with another peer-level apostle outside of the network and becomes accountable to that apostle. By way of illustration, if I may be personal, I lead a closed apostolic network of 25 apostles called Eagles Vision Apostolic Team. Each of these apostles, some of whom enjoy high public visibility, is accountable to me.

Although it is rare because of the relatively high water level of personal integrity among EVAT members, I have been called upon more than once to arbitrate disputes and even to receive and process accusations against EVAT members, which I am pleased, and hopefully equipped, to do.

CONCLUSION

I think it is clear that we are now in the midst of one of those historic Antioch seasons in which God is transitioning us from old paradigms to new paradigms. These changes will not go smoothly unless the players are covered with a blanket of sincere, informed, and powerful intercession. The enemy will attempt to block God's new season in every way possible, but prophetic intercession can neutralize his power and clear the way for the America of tomorrow and for the church of tomorrow.

My hope is that God's will be done on earth as it is in heaven!

C. Peter Wagner is president of Global Harvest Ministries (www.globalharvest.org), chancellor of Wagner Leadership Institute and presiding apostle of the International Coalition of Apostles. He has written numerous books, including *Dominion!* (ChosenBooks)

Notes

1. C. Peter Wagner, *The Book of Acts: A Commentary* (Ventura CA: Regal Books, 2008), 220-238.

2. Personal correspondence from Chuck Pierce, November 7, 2012.

3. Wolfgang Simson, "Our dear America—where do you go from here?", November 7, 2012, emailed from wolfsimson@compuserve.com.

4. Chuck D. Pierce, *God's Unfolding Battle Plan: A Field Manual for Advancing the Kingdom of God* (Ventura CA: Regal books, 2007), 211-216.

5. Chuck Pierce, "The Sleeping Giant Awakens." Email from Glory of Zion International, July 25, 2012, 1.

6. Pierce, *God's Unfolding Battle Plan*, 212.

7. David B. Barrett and Todd M. Johnson, World *Christian Trends AD30-AD2200* (Pasadena CA: William Carey Library, 2001), 543.

CHAPTER 14

SIX PRAYERS THAT CHANGE THE WORLD

by Julia Loren, with Bill Johnson, Heidi Baker, Brennan Manning, F.F. Bosworth, Mahesh Chavda, and Leanne Payne

These days call for intentional, focused prayer—to steady our nerves when we see destruction coming near and to overcome our fear to rise up in faith and love and power. We must have our relationship with Jesus so settled that we can sleep through any storm, knowing that His love and protection covers us. And we must also know that Jesus extended that love to us—before we were even saved. We are still living in the day of grace that began with the atonement and resurrection of Christ and extends until the *very last day* when Jesus returns.

How you perceive the nature and character of God determines how you pray and reveals your heart.

PREPARING YOUR MIND AND HEART FOR THE DAYS TO COME

Suffering is a mystery. Death is an enemy. No one knows this better than Jesus and even He doubted the goodness of the Father for a moment on the cross when He cried out, "My Father, why have You forsaken me?"

If we focus on suffering, we miss out on joy. If we focus on disaster, we miss out on living life abundantly. If we focus on the face and presence of Jesus and learn to focus there—first—when pain and loss strikes like a cobra, we will learn to rise above circumstances and live from the perspective of heaven. But we must be willing to set our minds on Christ and learn to see as He sees, love as He loves, and dwell in Him on a daily basis, practicing living in His presence and setting our minds on His goodness. We must learn to access the promise of living life abundantly—no matter what is going on around us! How do we access this higher life? Through prayer and meditation. Prayer prepares the mind and enlarges the heart. Prayer also connects us with the heart and mind of Christ. It is in that place of prayer, wrapped up in the presence of God, where the questions and emotions that assault our thought life surrender to His deep peace and rest. And when we learn to operate from a place of peace, learning to calm the storms of our hearts and minds, we can take authority over any storm around us.

Warriors prepare for battle by practicing what is called "battle-mindedness"—a deliberate setting of the mind to respond and react in a certain way under fire, knowing that others may be killed alongside of you but you can rise above the carnage to act according to training, and afterward process the resulting grief and loss in light of your mission. For the Christian, "battle-mindedness" involves knowing that in this world we will have tribulation and we choose to live unoffended by the ways of God and ways of the nature of our planet. We become comfortable with mystery and realize that suffering is a part of life—after the fall—and something that we can transcend with Christ who overcame the world. Our mission is to live in Christ and to live "out" Christ—extending His love to others.

I watch missionaries like Mother Theresa and Heidi Baker for signs of how they process the pain and suffering of the world while daily going out to deliberately meet it. They survived by setting the cornerstone of their theology (core value of battle-mindedness) on one simple Scripture—God is Love. And they focus on seeing the face of Christ in everyone they meet. They see redemption, not judgment. They see divine purpose and potential in each person they stop and touch. They lay the horrific images of the ravages of sin and death evident in peoples' bodies at the foot of the cross and worship their way past the suffering until they feel the lift of the Spirit of God enabling them to rise into the beauty realm of heaven, and rest there, in His presence. It is a rest they have learned to access in the midst of the chaos and needs swirling around them. They developed, through discipline, a form of "battle-mindedness" that enabled them to live unoffended and walk about focused on Christ.

This is the place of total surrender—living in the God who is Love. And here is where the Church can live full of the light and glory of God. Are you ready? Neither am I. But let's get on with it.

PRAYERS THAT CHANGE OUR WORLD

Several of my favorite teachers reveal the nature and character of God and offer thoughts on how to intentionally approach prayer during these tumultuous times. Bill Johnson, Pastor of Bethel Church in Redding, California, speaks about Jesus, God of forgiveness and reconciliation. Brennan Manning, a former Catholic priest, writes about the tenderness of Jesus. Heidi Baker, international missionary, speaks to the love revolution we can start. F.F. Bosworth, author of the classic work *Christ the Healer*, writes about the compassion of Jesus. Mahesh Chavda, an apostolic minister in South Carolina, writes about passing on the power of your testimony. Leanne Payne, pastor care forerunner and prophet, writes about God's ability to love the world through you.

They all offer us ways to pray about the future based on the perception that God is good. Prayer should release something into the atmosphere to create change. If we align ourselves first with the heart and will of a good God, we are able to pray the prayers of faith that release the transformational presence and power of God into any situation—personally, locally, or even globally. Praying about the things that God shows you is a privilege given to the favored of God—us. Do we pray to extend judgment or blessing? What is the heart of God? Let's take hold of the heart of God and release the nature of God into the world through intercessory prayers and actions.

RELEASING THE FORGIVENESS AND FAVOR OF THE LORD

By Bill Johnson, from May 2011 Leaders Advance, Bethel Church

> *So Jesus said to them again, "Peace be with you; as the Father has sent Me, I also send you." And when He had said this, He breathed on them and said to them, "Receive the Holy Spirit. If you forgive the sins of any, their sins have been forgiven them; if you retain the sins of any, they have been retained"* (John 20:21-23 NASB).

> *Now all these things are from God, who reconciled us to Himself through Christ and gave us the ministry of reconciliation, namely, that God was in Christ reconciling the world to Himself, not counting their trespasses against them, and He has committed to us the word of reconciliation* (2 Corinthians 5:18-19 NASB).

Forgiveness and reconciliation means that we do not hold a sin against someone, that we do not keep a record. What happens in these cities and nations of the world is that the Church has kept a full record of their sins. Statements have been made that God must judge.

I think we need to live with an appreciation for what has changed in the last decades. The righteous are getting sprinkled into every system. The church wants to call down judgment on Hollywood because they're doing stupid things, causing many to stumble, and yet the Lord has anointed prophets to go into the chambers of the King and they are there right now. Why judge now? How about 40 years ago when no one was there? That would have been a great time because there was no one interceding on their behalf. Now He has worked people into the system. Is this when they should be judged?

This is when the entire thing can be changed and shifted because we have people of righteous influence in places of leadership....

There are nations that are under prophetic unction where the leaders of the nation are consulting the prophets of the Lord to know what to do in crisis. So why would the Lord wipe them out right now? It is like planting a crop, waiting until it is almost ready for harvest, and then burning it down. It makes no sense.

We have been given a ministry of reconciliation, which means I look at Las Vegas and I do not accuse them in my heart. I take no pleasure in the tragedy that happens there or in Japan, a materialistic world. How about standing up and saying, "Lord, You've had such favor on us; please extend the favor you've given to us on them."

The Lord waits for this stuff. Sin requires judgment—there is no question. But He put a clause in there, "Hey, if somebody will stand in the gap and contend for them, plead for their case... what I am looking for is for My delegated ones to take responsibility and do what they are supposed to do, and cry out for the favor given to them to be extended to this undeserving group. I forgive them. I do not hold their sins against them."

Intercession has taken on an accusational nature and it is not intercession. It is co-laboring with the accuser.

Intercession is to stand before the Lord and say, "You've give me favor and I did not deserve it on my best day; now I am asking—show the same favor toward this city. Show the same favor toward this person."

Whoever you forgive, I forgive.

When we read of these atrocities, the sex trades, the homosexuality that runs rampant and all this craziness that is all over the world, is our first reaction, "God, we need to purge this country of that evil"? Because He gave us the greatest invitation imaginable—whoever you forgive, I forgive.

RELEASING THE TENDERNESS OF GOD

By Brennan Manning, excerpted from The Wisdom of Tenderness

As Christians living in the Spirit, we're called to pass on the tenderness of God. The parameters of our compassion extend beyond those who opt for our lifestyle, favor our existence, or make us feel good. Charges of elitism are dropped for the lack of evidence. Peace and reconciliation for all, without exception—even for moral failures—is the radical lifestyle of Christians living in the wisdom of accepted tenderness. We may be called friends of tax collectors and sinners—but only because we are (or should be). We understand that we are in the company of some rather honorable people, those sinners; in fact, we in the company of Jesus Himself. According to the gospel, it's unrestrained tenderness and limitless compassion that stamp our relationship with the Father of Jesus as belonging to the order of the Really Real.

The Lord is in the people with whom we rub shoulders every day, the people whom we think we can read as an open book. Sometimes He's buried there, sometimes He's bound hand and foot there, but He's there. We've been given the gift of faith to detect His presence there, and the Holy Spirit has been poured out into our hearts that we may love Him there. For the meaning of our religion is love. Christianity is all about loving, and we either take it or leave it. It's not about worship and morality, except insofar as these things are expressions of the love that causes them both.

RELEASING GOD'S MERCY AND COMPASSION

By F.F. Bosworth, excerpted from Christ the Healer

God is not anything so much as He is love. The most conspicuous statements in the Scriptures about our heavenly Father are the declarations concerning His love, His mercy, His compassion. There is no note that can be sounded concerning God's character that will so inspire faith as this one. In our revivals, I've seen faith rise "mountain high" when the truth of God's present love and compassion began to draw upon the minds and hearts of the people. It is not what God *can* do but what we know He *yearns* to do that inspires faith.

By showing His compassion everywhere in the healing of the sick, Jesus unveiled the compassionate heart of God to the people, and the multitudes came to Him for help. Oh, how insidiously has Satan worked to hide this glorious fact from the people. He has broadcasted the unscriptural, illogical, and worn-out statement that the age of miracles is past, until he has almost succeeded in eclipsing the compassion of God from the eyes of the world. Modern theology magnifies the *power* of God more than it magnifies His *compassion*; his power more than it does the great fact that "the exceeding greatness of His power [is] to *usward.*" In no place does the Bible say that "God is power," but it *does* say that "God is *love.*" It is not faith in God's power that secures His blessings, but faith in His love and in His will.

RELEASING THE GOODNESS OF GOD

By Mahesh Chavda, excerpted from
The Hidden Power of the Blood of Jesus

As believers, we each have a personal testimony to God's goodness and faithfulness, and to the power of the Passover

Lamb to cleanse us from sin. God wants us to pass on our testimony to generation after generation so that the knowledge of Him becomes personal to each of our sons and daughters so that they can take possession of the Passover Lamb for themselves....

Our children need to hear us say, "This is what the Lord did for me." Lost people need to hear us say it. When we give voice to our personal experience with the saving grace of God, we encourage others to believe that His grace is for them as well.

The more we testify of the Lord's goodness to us, the more He will build up our testimony. He will continue to bless us, giving us more to testify about. His hand will be over us in our lives, in our children's lives, in our homes, in our financial lives, in our business lives, and in our creative lives.

RELEASING THE LOVE OF GOD TO THE WORLD

By Leanne Payne, excerpted from Listening Prayer

Many years ago I heard of Dr. Bob Pierce, the founder of World Vision, sobbing with his arms outstretched around a large globe of the world. He was praying for the orphaned children of the world. God entrusted him with a special mission in regard to them, and his vision was in line with God's—it was global. He had acquired the Lord's mind on how to pray and how to follow up on those prayers.

This habit of Dr. Pierce's made such a deep impression on me that I now always keep a globe at hand. On first hearing of his custom, I could hardly imagine that God could use me globally. But throwing my arms around a globe, I cried out for God to somehow, in some way, love this needy planet through me. "Lord, love Your world through me" is the prayer that has been with me ever since....

Christ died for all who will come to Him; His redemptive plan is global. We are to go into all the world—in our prayers. Then we are all the more effective in prayer for the needs closer at hand.

HEIDI BAKER

Everywhere we go I see people getting completely wrecked. But I feel like God wants to bring this radical-like love revolution where people start focusing on loving the one right in front of them, and it's more about carrying love everywhere than it's about a meeting.

This movement that I'm praying for is a love revolution where Christians are actually known by their love wherever they are in society, wherever they move, wherever they walk. It's all about breathing, smelling, and walking like Jesus, not so much about a meeting in a certain place. It's like carrying His presence, the glory of His love out into every single part of society. Where people don't have to ask who you believe in. Because of the way you treat people and care for people they can see who you believe in. Christians are known by their love. And I feel like God is ripping anger out of people, and depression, and fear, and causing them to live a life of radical love. That's what I'm seeing. That's what I'm longing for.

It is sovereign when God takes our little hearts and makes them bigger—actually a gift. There's something that when God does that, when He comes crashing in on you in a sovereign way in a meeting, then He totally takes away hatred and anger and allows you to forgive people who have hurt you and ridiculed you. Once that happens you change, but then you have to live that life out.

I believe that we need more of those kinds of meetings where the presence is so strong that God literally rips out the hardness of our hearts and puts His heart in us. That's what I'm longing for, more of those meetings. I said it during a meeting in South Korea not long ago. I saw South Koreans come forward and instead of just writhing and shaking to receive the anointing and wanting the woman or man of power to touch them, they were on their faces sobbing their guts out because God was giving them a taste of His huge heart for them.

So now, my friends, go out and change the world!

ABOUT JULIA LOREN

Julia Loren is the author of more than a dozen books focusing on the present move of God including the Shifting Shadows trilogy: *Shifting Shadows of Supernatural Power*, (with contributors Bill Johnson and Mahesh Chavda), *Shifting Shadows of Supernatural Experiences* (co-authored by James Goll), and *Supernatural Anointing*. She is also a counselor and life coach and ministers in churches and in retreats around the world, assisting communities and individuals to understand the times we live in and receive an encounter with God who will launch them into their sacred destinies. She lives on an island north of Seattle, Washington but is often spotted soaking up the sun in her native land of California.

For more information see:
www.julialoren.com
www.globalshorescounseling.com